HARDY ROSES

THE ESSENTIAL GUIDE FOR HIGH LATITUDES AND ALTITUDES

Third Edition

HARDY ROSES

THE ESSENTIAL GUIDE FOR HIGH LATITUDES AND ALTITUDES

Bob Osborne

with photographs by Beth Powning

FIREFLY BOOKS

A FIREFLY BOOK

Published by Firefly Books Ltd. 2020
Copyright © 2020 Firefly Books Ltd.
Text copyright © 2020 Bob Osborne
Photographs copyright © 2020 Beth Powning, except as listed below.

First printing

Library of Congress Control Number: 2019952852

Library and Archives Canada Cataloguing in Publication
Title: Hardy roses : the essential guide for high latitudes and altitudes / Bob Osborne
with photographs by Beth Powning.
Names: Osborne, Robert A., 1949- author. | Powning, Beth, 1949- photographer.
Description: Third edition. | Includes bibliographical references and index.
Identifiers: Canadiana 20190208848 | ISBN 9780228102434 (softcover)
Subjects: LCSH: Rose culture—Canada. | LCSH: Roses—Varieties.
Classification: LCC SB411 .O73 2020 | DDC 635.9/336440971—dc23

Published in the United States by	Published in Canada by
Firefly Books (U.S.) Inc.	Firefly Books Ltd.
P.O. Box 1338, Ellicott Station	50 Staples Avenue, Unit 1
Buffalo, New York 14205	Richmond Hill, Ontario L4B 0A7

Cover and interior design: Hartley Millson and Noor Majeed
Editor: Julie Takasaki
Illustrations: George A. Walker
Map on page 178 © Her Majesty the Queen in Right of Canada, as represented by the
    Minister of Natural Resources, 2014
Map on page 179 Courtesy of USDA Agricultural Research Service; map data © Oregon
    State University (OSU)

Printed in Korea

Canada [∎∎] We acknowledge the financial support of the Government of Canada.

Additional photo credits:
Bob Osborne: 132 (bottom), 161
David Austin Roses, www.davidaustinroses.com: 110 (top)
Helen Curwood/Shutterstock: 127
Luc Pouliot/Shutterstock: 58
Manfred Ruckszio/Alamy Stock Photo: 22 (left), 150
Nancy Kennedy/Shutterstock: 57
Nigel Cattlin/Alamy Stock Photo: 62, 64, 65
PaleCloudedWhite/Wikimedia Commons (https:
    //commons.wikimedia.org/wiki/File:Crown_gall
    _on_rose_(b).JPG): 63
Paroli Galperti/REDA &CO srl/Alamy Stock Photo: 155
R Ann Kautzky/Alamy Stock Photo: 154 (bottom), 170

CONTENTS

◄ This bumblebee is one of the many insects that pollinate roses, unwittingly transferring pollen from flower to flower in its search for food.

Introduction to the Third Edition

Those who are familiar with the first and second editions will notice substantial changes in this new edition. I have edited the text by incorporating corrections and clarifications. I have also changed the positioning of the roses in various sections, and made some adjustments in the descriptions that reflect my evolving experience. Additionally, I have omitted a few roses that appeared in the previous editions while adding a number of new roses.

The roses in this book are those my nursery has grown for decades, or at least several years for newer cultivars. We believe their performance shows them capable of growing in cold country gardens, or gardens anywhere. There are many roses not covered in these pages that can be grown in northern climates, but I am confident that this list offers the northern grower a great number of superb, diverse roses from which to choose.

You will also note my use of the word "cultivar" rather than "variety" when referring to the roses. Although variety is more commonly used, in truth it refers to a group of individuals that are similar but not genetically identical. Good examples of varieties would be peas or beans. When you plant the seeds of a named variety of pea, each seedling is similar to the other, yet each is slightly different on a genetic level. A cultivar is a unique individual whose characteristics are maintained by the process of clonal propagation, either by cuttings or by grafting on a rootstock. In an effort to conform to horticultural standards, I have adopted the term cultivar to denote what many refer to as a variety. In another nod to proper botanical terms, I will refer to "prickles," which is the correct name for what many call "thorns."

Nearly all of the photos were taken in a garden that does not use insecticides. They may sometimes show damage due to various insects that attack specific cultivars.

Preface

For me, a garden is a place of discovery, learning and wonder. Each time I walk the paths of my garden, everything is different. I might be wrapped in a sweater and parka scrunching though the snow or sweating on a hot summer day. I might be bathed in the light of a soft, pink sunrise mirrored by countless leaves or blinded by the intense sun at zenith, its power wilting a thirsty rose. Perhaps a low fog hangs amid the trees, muffling the sounds of the garden's inhabitants, or a tempest is tearing leaves from limbs.

The tapestry of a garden constantly changes. The muted tones of winter flow into the spectral riots of spring and summer, and then on into earthen fall. The plants grow wider and higher, break and split, flower and fruit. Spiders wait on dew-hung threads to strike, bees hover between blossoms, and birds sweep and call. Shafts of light break through the trees, and the patterns dance across the ground.

Gardens are planted and nurtured by our efforts. Our ideas mold gardens into forms, but a humbling magic transforms them into something greater than the sum of their parts and beyond our initial dreams. We create worlds when we create gardens. A shrub becomes a haven for a bird. The bird eats a caterpillar on a fruit tree. The bird's droppings nourish microorganisms in the soil, and the fine root hairs of a rose absorb the chemical residues left by the decomposing bodies of those organisms and transforms them into colorful flowers. Every event triggers other events.

To be a spectator of this fascinating interaction is my greatest reward as a gardener. I revel in the variety of expectations and sensations that a garden offers. The limitless possibilities can overwhelm me as well, and I have to discipline myself to choose avenues of exploration that most appeal to me. After having had countless "favorite" plants, I have abandoned the notion of awarding special status. Each of them is unique and exciting. The rose is not my favorite plant, but one that gives me special pleasures and challenges.

Each garden is restricted by its site and climate. You can stretch these limits at times, but not understanding them will lead to failures. My garden is located in New Brunswick, Canada, where winter temperatures can drop to –40°F (–40°C). The firm grip of midwinter can be broken by a mild storm bred in the ocean only to be re-established with intensity as arctic winds push back the warmth. It is a climate that demands endurance and patience both of the gardener and of the plants.

Introducing roses into such a garden seemed a daunting task when I began. The trepidation I felt initially has blossomed into an exhilaration that has me spellbound, not only by the measure of success we have enjoyed, but also by the sheer variety of color, shape, texture and fragrance that this extraordinary group of plants offers. By accepting the limitations of our cold winters, I was forced to look beyond the more usual offerings of roses — the hybrid teas, the grandifloras, the floribundas — and toward those roses that are less common.

A forsythia blooms in the spring for a brief but glorious two weeks. Even though its flowers are short lived, we treasure it as one of spring's harbingers. Daylily blossoms last less than 24 hours before they are shriveled and done, yet we cannot imagine summer without them. A close examination of a potentilla flower reveals not extravagance but a refined simplicity. Yet, when we see the bush covered with these simple flowers, the effect is overwhelming. We accept these for themselves and find places for them in our gardens. However, when "shrub roses" are mentioned, many gardeners say, "Oh, you mean wild roses" or, "Don't they only have five petals?" If you have passed over the world of hardy shrub roses for these reasons, or if you do not know anything about them, be ready to be enveloped by their beauty and variety.

Any gardener can use and appreciate hardy roses, but many see the rose as a symbol of frustration as well as beauty. They may have spent countless hours trying to protect their roses from the ravages of winter, only to be left with crumbling blackened stems in the spring. Others never try roses because they have heard how difficult they are to grow. This book is an attempt to provide these gardeners with information. Proper nurturing and, more importantly, proper choice of cultivar can mean the difference between aggravation and exhilarating success.

It is my desire to convey a heartfelt love of these roses. At the same time, I want to emphasize the need for objectivity in choosing cultivars best suited to the requirements of both the site and the gardener's needs. All these roses are lovely, but all have at least some weaknesses. It is important to define these weaknesses. Therefore, I have strived to give a balanced and accurate description of the roses.

Words cannot replace a good picture when it comes to plant descriptions. Beth Powning's photographs are meant to portray each rose's characteristics as accurately as possible. By their artistry, however, the photos transcend this purpose, allowing the viewer to revel in the grace and beauty of each curved petal and the endless shadings of color that make roses so exciting and rewarding to grow.

Special thanks to Freeman Patterson. I would like to acknowledge Frank Leith Skinner's fascinating book *Horticultural Horizons: Plant Breeding and Introduction at Dropmore, Manitoba*, from which I excerpted his discussion of the origin of the rose F.J. Grootendorst. I would also like to acknowledge the help of Valerie Ahwee, Brian Dykemann, Catherine Venart, Sue Hooper, Mike Lowe, Julie Takasaki, Suzie Verrier and the many gardeners who have offered their wisdom and advice. Walking alone is nice, but walking with someone of like interests doubles the pleasure.

— Bob Osborne

PART 1

HARDY ROSES: THE FLOWERING OF A DREAM

◀ Alexander Mackenzie is a good example of a rose that combines hardiness, repeat blooming and disease resistance.

1

CREATING TAPESTRIES

◀ Here, a northern gardener's dream has been transformed into a tapestry as sumptuous as any through the use of tough winter-hardy roses.

Gardens are as personal as their creators and are as varied in style, composition and detailing as gardeners are in their hopes, aspirations and temperaments. This is as it should be. One of the great joys for any plant lover is to walk through others' gardens. Each garden is unique and conveys something of the creator's dreams and interests. I knew of a small perennial garden on a windswept hill tended by a wonderfully selfless and charming gentleman who devoted his later life to the study of hardy perennials. His garden had no fancy statues, no carefully contoured or planned beds; it simply flowed across the landscape as the roots of a plant might work their way through the soil. It was an unassuming, gentle and kindly place. It reflected the very best of this good man.

Although this garden was unstructured, it worked. A garden that works, no matter the style, does so because its creator understands the nature of the plants in it. Each plant is unique, having a certain size, color and texture. A creeping phlox grows only a few inches tall; its fine moss-like leaves are a living carpet. In the cool, early weeks of spring, its small, five-petaled blossoms

Scharlachglut is a large, arching shrub with very large blooms.

weave their alluring patterns of white, pink, red or blue. The red oak tree, beginning as a lowly acorn, grows to dominate a landscape. Its broad, strong branches thrust out from a massive trunk of deeply furrowed, smoky bark. The leaves, large and pointed, lose their glossy green in the fall, turn to smoldering red, bleach to camel brown and then hang persistently until the snow's weight or winter's storms scatter them onto the ground.

Just as you would never think of using an oak where a phlox would be more appropriate, you should use similar care in choosing roses. Whether you are creating a reproduction of Versailles, an English cottage garden or a garden that you build as you go along, if you do not have an understanding of your plants' vital needs and statistics, the results may disappoint you. With some care and forethought, however, it is easy to create gardens that work without any limitations on your style.

Roses come in every size, shape, color and texture. For example, Scharlachglut is a vigorous, wide bush with velvety, deep red single blooms that are often as wide as a hand, whereas Double Scotch White is a dense bush with fine foliage and dainty white blooms that are a bit larger than a thumbnail. It is difficult to imagine two more different roses. They evoke totally different feelings and have different space requirements, yet each is enchanting. As the gardener, your task is to place these roses in the garden, so that each can grow to its potential and at the same time not interfere with either the growth of other plants or the visual arrangement you are constructing.

Hardy roses are a delightfully varied group of plants. Many of them, overshadowed by their aristocratic cousins, were known only to a small group of astute gardeners. As they become more available, and as gardeners' horizons expand, this vast array of plants we group together as "shrub roses" will soon take its rightful place among its peers. Designing with hardy roses is an exciting challenge, one limited only by your space, determination and imagination.

The terminology of hardy roses is confusing. Hardy roses, meaning those able to tolerate very cold temperatures, are most often referred to as "shrub roses." However, the term is also used to mean a rose having a full and generally vigorous appearance. Be warned that not all shrubby roses are hardy, and not all hardy roses are shrubby in appearance. To add to the confusion, many people refer to old-fashioned roses as shrubs, and others refer to any roses other than hybrid teas or floribundas as shrubs. No one has yet unraveled this maze of definitions to everyone's satisfaction, so in order to avoid total exasperation, let common sense be your guide.

Roses have a rather special place in the history of gardens. More often than not they have been treated somewhat like gems in need of a crown. Many older European gardens devoted a separate section to roses. Often geometric, these rose gardens rarely contained much else

Double Scotch White is a dense plant sporting small globular flowers with a rich fragrance — quite the contrast to Scharlachglut.

in the way of plants. They were designed to dazzle the observer with the shape, color and fragrance exclusively of roses.

In the past century rose growers of the world have fixed most of their attentions on the group known collectively as hybrid teas. Generally speaking, these roses are grown to show off their extravagant and captivating flowers. Often the plant itself has been somewhat disregarded or even ignored in the breeding process. As a result, many of these beautiful flowers grow on rather spindly, disease-prone bushes.

The recent revival of interest in shrub roses reflects a changing attitude toward the rose's place in modern gardens. This trend has been convenient for the northern gardener, as many of the hardiest roses belong to several species commonly used before the advent of hybrid teas, floribundas and grandifloras, and are quite hardy. Because these shrubs have become more popular again, their availability has increased dramatically. The increased interest in shrub roses has also spurred many rose breeders to create shrub roses with longer flowering periods, increased hardiness and disease resistance. The rose garden will never be the same.

More gardeners are integrating the rose into mixtures of plant species. The vigorous *Rosa rugosa* roses are becoming backgrounds for perennial borders. Low bedding roses are mixed with low shrubs or annuals. The combinations are endless. The shrub roses, with their solidity and varied textures, are choice plants, but the promoter of shrub roses still faces a challenge. The name "rose" has come to be synonymous with hybrid tea and to a lesser extent floribunda and grandiflora. If shown a shrub rose, many gardeners will refuse to acknowledge it as a "real" rose. It does not fit their image of what a rose should be. Because the shrub roses are a fantastically diverse group of plants, a great deal of education is necessary to show the diverse uses these plants can have. Once gardeners realize that this wide array of plants offers an exciting challenge to their designing talents, these roses will assume an importance unprecedented in their history.

When planted in masses, shrub roses can steal the show from most other plants. The sight of 20 or 30 mature roses in full bloom covering a bed or carpeting a hillside can even stir the heart of a confirmed rhododendron enthusiast. Granted not every home has the space to house such an extravagance of roses, but it is well worth considering when trying to decide how to deal with open spaces. It is important to emphasize maintenance during the first few years, but once grown together, a group of shrub roses takes minimal care and will repay you with an annual display of color that has the power to wash away your burdens and reaffirm the reason you till the earth.

Shrub roses can, of course, be given their own space in the garden. With a careful arrangement of height, form and color, a spectacular area can be created for roses only. Particularly for the collector of cultivars, these "rooms" can provide an area to study, compare and admire. It is worth remembering that if you are planting roses that are not recurrent bloomers, it may be effective to include plants that will be in flower when the roses are not or perhaps some recurrent cultivars of roses, so that no section of the garden is left colorless for months at a time.

One of our nursery's entrances is the perfect spot for ▶ Frü Dagmar Hastrup — a selection of *Rosa rugosa* that combines hardiness, vigor, fragrance, repeat blooming and great fall foliage.

2 WINTERING

Beams of sunlight reflect off the warm pink petals of a rose hugging a rocky crag high on a hill in the far north. The steady, cold winds of winter have pressed its stems against the stones, so they barely rise above them. A month after its fleeting petals are torn away by wind, the first frost coats its leaves. By midwinter the stems are frozen so deeply that a casual touch will shatter them like glass. Yet under the higher sun of spring, new shoots push from swollen buds, and another year's cycle of growth begins.

Farther south, a gardener pokes through her carefully constructed mound of mulch to discover her rose has become a blackened skeleton. All the effort spent in trying to protect the rose from what she imagined was a mild winter has been wasted. How can one rose survive tortuous, frigid winter conditions, while the other dies when faced with much warmer winter temperatures? The answer lies in a wondrous process called supercooling.

◄ This is the stunning fall foliage of Frü Dagmar Hastrup, the last hurrah before the frigid temperatures of winter set in.

If you magnified a plant cell, it would, more or less, resemble a box. The outside of the box is the cell membrane. This rigid structure holds the various fluids and complex structures within its walls as well as gives the cell its strength. As fall approaches, plants that have the ability undergo an amazing change. Shorter daylight hours and falling temperatures trigger the cell to reduce the amount of water within it, until all that remains is an extremely thin film of water around the important structures inside the cell. A little-known property of water is its ability to remain elastic well below the freezing point when it is a very thin film. This means that no ice crystals form (ice crystals would rupture and destroy the cell), and the cell can survive extremely low temperatures.

Each plant differs in its resistance to ice formation. The hardiest plants can survive in temperatures as low as –40°F (–40°C). This is the cutoff temperature for most hardy deciduous plants, although a few evergreens and deciduous plants can take virtually all the water in their cells and put it outside the cell wall, in the spaces between the cells. You can find these plants growing well into the arctic tundra.

Our super hardy rose hugging its cold, rocky bit of earth belongs to those roses that, through countless generations, have developed the ability to use the supercooling process to its limit. The more tender rose has been subjected to temperatures below what it can tolerate, and the expanding ice crystals have quite literally torn its cells apart. It is the challenge of the northern gardener to discover which roses are the masters of supercooling.

A look at the various rose species can be an important aid in deciding which will be worth growing in cold climates. Within a given species there is usually a good deal of genetic diversity. Plants differ as we do in characteristics. If a rose species is growing in an area where low temperatures occur, those individuals with a greater ability to use the process of supercooling will be more likely to survive, and therefore to pass that ability on to their offspring. In time, this gradual selection process allows species to move northward into even colder areas.

Consider the tender hybrid teas. Although a complex group, these roses were developed primarily from *Rosa chinensis*, a species found in southern China. In its native habitat it rarely encounters temperatures below the freezing point. Thus, there has been little selection pressure toward the creation of individuals that could tolerate extremes of cold. When growing roses that are derived from species such as *Rosa chinensis* in gardens with severe winters, the chances for successful overwintering are very poor without special protection.

The roses that are successful in northern gardens are derived from species that have been able to adjust to difficult winter conditions through the process of mutation and adaptation. They have become adept at supercooling. Although a large number of species are relatively hardy, some have played a vital role in the breeding of hardy roses.

Our best cultivars have been selected from these species or have been hybridized using these species as sources of hardiness. When choosing a rose for your garden, try to find out to which species (or mix of species) the rose belongs. If it comes from one of the following, it means that it comes from a group with good winter survival skills.

ROSA ALBA

The most expensive perfume in the world pales in comparison to the scent of a single bloom from a *Rosa alba*. This ancient species has a special place in rose history and a very precious place in northern gardens. Although little has been done with *Rosa alba* by modern breeders, the older cultivars available to us are invaluable. They are generally very healthy, and most are hardy in Zone 4. Some can be grown into Zone 3. Nearly all come in shades of white and pink. Because they are not repeat bloomers, they have been relegated to the background of the rose world since the introduction of the perpetual bloomers and the hybrid teas, but I would no more give up my *Rosa albas* than I would my azaleas, which bloom for a much briefer time.

ROSA CENTIFOLIA

Peter Beales, in his excellent book *Classic Roses*, tells us that *Rosa centifolia* is not really a species, but a complex of hybrids comprised of genes from *Rosa gallica*, *Rosa canina*, *Rosa moschata* and others. Be this as it may, the Cabbage Rose, as it is known, contains a number of older forms that are both interesting and hardy. Among these are the curious moss roses. These novelties have innumerable small prickles that feel more like soft bristles that cover the stems and buds.

Alba Maxima is an ancient and venerated rose.

The diminutive blooms of Striped Moss, a hardy *Rosa centifolia*, are rarely seen in gardens today.

Persian Yellow is a rose whose legacy lives on in nearly all hardy yellow roses.

Alain Blanchard is a good and unique representative of the *Rosa gallicas*.

ROSA FOETIDA

The double form of this species, Persian Yellow, figures importantly in the breeding of most yellow roses and is the progenitor of nearly all hardy yellow cultivars that have been developed. Considering it is native to southwest Asia, it is an amazingly hardy species, surviving even into Zone 3. Its weakness, however, is a susceptibility to the fungal disease blackspot.

ROSA GALLICA

This species is currently enjoying a resurgence of popularity after having been sadly neglected for nearly a century. Many important cultivars were produced in the early and mid-19th century, and these still form the majority of available cultivars in the species. However, modern breeders such as David Austin and Peter Beales of England have introduced some stunning new shrub roses with *Rosa gallica* in their blood. Most of the *gallicas* are quite hardy and come in a profusion of colors, including dark tones as in Cardinal de Richelieu, whose flowers are a deep, rich purple. Most have strong perfume, and the flowers are very often double or very double, meaning that there are so many petals they often split into four quadrants of petals. Such roses are referred to as quartered roses.

ROSA RUGOSA

If you had to single out the most important species used in breeding for hardiness, it would have to be *Rosa rugosa*. This native of northern China and Japan has a number of important attributes. Paramount among its virtues is extreme hardiness. Many cultivars of *Rosa rugosa* will survive in Zone 2. The flowers of this species are usually large and fragrant, with colors varying from white through the range of pinks to mauve red. The coarse-textured foliage is unusually healthy. Blackspot and mildew rarely show up in this species. Lastly, its deep orangey-red hips add a decorative and useful accent to the plant in fall, and in addition they are edible and used for rose hip tea and jam.

My introduction to the world of hardy roses began with the purchase of a Blanc Double

Rosa spinosissima has been used to create many alluring ▶ roses, such as this Williams' Double.

Blanc Double de Coubert, one of the most famous *Rosa rugosa* hybrids, has pure white blooms.

ROSA SPINOSISSIMA (formerly ROSA PIMPINELLIFOLIA)

A species found growing in Europe and Asia, this rose became known as the Scotch rose. It was found natively in the British Isles, and a good deal of selection and breeding work were carried out in the 18th and 19th centuries in both Scotland and England. From this work arose numerous single and double cultivars in white and pink. Crossed with *Rosa foetida*, which had yellow flowers, it gave rise to several yellow forms as well, including Harison's Yellow and Williams' Double.

The small and delicate foliage of *Rosa spinosissima* is unusual. Its thin stems are armed with delicate-looking prickles that have a way of finding flesh. Generally, it flowers once in late spring or early summer, although many of its hybrids have repeat bloom. One of the better known is Stanwell Perpetual, whose blush pink blooms flower nonstop until frost.

de Coubert. Drinking in the sweet, heady fragrance of its first blooms addicted me to roses immediately. This was not a rose that needed to be pampered. It grew defiantly in the garden, scoffing at winter. Ever since discovering this superb ambassador of the *rugosas*, we have concentrated much of our effort on the many excellent hybrids of this species that are now available. If you are living in the very coldest regions, *Rosa rugosa* hybrids are some of the finest and hardiest.

3 NURTURING

Success with growing roses requires not magic but knowledge. If you understand the basic needs of your plants and ensure those needs are satisfied, then the magic we call growth can take place, and I can think of no more miraculous a process than the ability of a plant to use the sun's energy to turn water and carbon dioxide into sugar, the food that fuels growth. In order to make the most of this ability, you need to nurture your roses, to give them all the advantages you can. By providing a healthy soil, adequate water, lots of sun and enough room for growth, you can help your roses reach their potential. Your reward will be the goal of every rose grower — rainbows of sun-washed petals and perfumed evening walks.

◀ The cells in the leaves of this Polareis harness the energy of sunlight to fuel the growth of the plant.

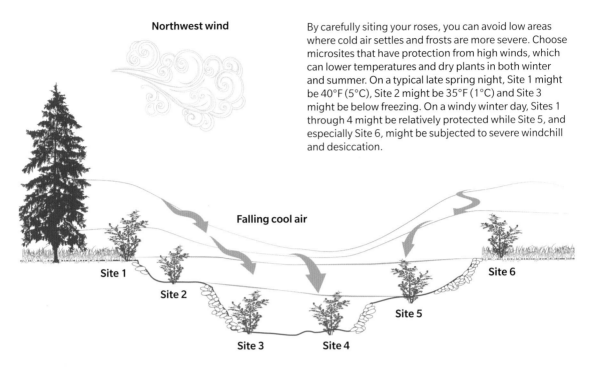

Northwest wind

By carefully siting your roses, you can avoid low areas where cold air settles and frosts are more severe. Choose microsites that have protection from high winds, which can lower temperatures and dry plants in both winter and summer. On a typical late spring night, Site 1 might be 40°F (5°C), Site 2 might be 35°F (1°C) and Site 3 might be below freezing. On a windy winter day, Sites 1 through 4 might be relatively protected while Site 5, and especially Site 6, might be subjected to severe windchill and desiccation.

Falling cool air

Site 1

Site 2

Site 3

Site 4

Site 5

Site 6

SITE

Before you can begin to think about the details of growing roses, you must first decide where you are going to plant them. This can be among your most important decisions. Unless you wish to move, you cannot change your climate. Your position on the globe will determine the general weather conditions and the hours of light available to you. Your particular site will also have a bearing on the garden. Sites differ in soil type, general wind exposure, overall air flow over the topography and, depending upon the size of the site, the alignment toward the sun. Urban environments may affect a site by altering such elements as air quality and light conditions. These are site constraints over which you have little control.

Within your site, however, there are often many "microsites." By changing your plant's position within a site, you can often alter the amount and quality of sunlight, the high and low temperatures, the exposure to wind, the water drainage or the soil composition.

When you are deciding where to dig the hole, remember that roses need sunlight. The amount of sunlight will affect plant vigor, flower production and disease susceptibility. The best situation for a rose is one that receives full sun from dawn to dusk. Many gardens will not be able to provide this, but try to maximize sun exposure. Roses growing in partial shade will usually be spindly and stingy with their flowers. Most roses growing in full shade will slowly die. Sunlight is also an important deterrent to fungal growth. A good dose of sun is far more effective for prevention of mildew or rust than any amount of sprays.

Although we think of ourselves as living in a particular hardiness zone (see the Zone Maps on pages 178–79), many sites may contain several microsites that may differ as much as a full zone. The choice of a microsite can greatly affect winter survival. For example, a grove of trees will block the prevailing wind. In winter, a rose planted with this protection would suffer far less from cold, dry winds. These winds can injure a plant by dehydrating it even though the temperature may not be that low. A change in elevation can also be important. On those cold, still nights in spring or fall, frost will form in low pockets, where the heavier cold air settles. Higher areas will not be as cold and may escape the frost.

Likewise, soil conditions can differ drastically between microsites. Roses are particularly sensitive to wet soils. If their roots sit in water for any length of time, the roots will die from lack of oxygen. In winter, wet soils are colder. Even if the roots might have enough oxygen to survive, low temperatures in winter may spell disaster because when the water in the soil turns to ice, it conducts cold through the soil better than a more aerated soil. It is essential that your site be well drained. If you must plant in a wet area, install drain tile below the root zone, and direct this water away from the plants to a lower area such as a swale or ditch. Filling the bottom of a hole with gravel does not solve a drainage problem. If there is no way for the water to escape, the root zone will still fill up with water, and your rose will suffer as much damage as if there had been no gravel.

The texture and richness of soils will often vary dramatically, even in a fairly small area. If possible, choose an area with a deep, rich topsoil. If there is no such spot, or if your choice of site is guided by other limits, do not despair. Soil is something you can work with to improve.

SOIL

Plants use the soil for anchorage and for sustenance. The soil in which your rose is planted will, in large measure, determine how well your rose grows. A basic understanding of how soil works is essential in managing your garden. Soil is not simply a medium on which to pour bags of fertilizer. Rather, soils are complex, dynamic, living systems that react to the changes we create. The processes we use in gardening initiate changes that affect the soil and therefore our plants.

Nearly every rose book ever written says that roses must have a clay soil to grow to perfection. This emphasis on clay soils is misleading. Clay is recommended partially because of its ability to hold more water, thus making it less likely that the rose will dry out. Dry rosebushes do not flower or grow well. Clay soils are generally more nutrient rich than sandy soils as well. Another reason clay soils are recommended is because virtually all roses in the past, and most even today, are propagated by budding the desired cultivar onto a rootstock. Usually the rootstock is either *Rosa multiflora* or *Rosa canina*, species that grow best in heavier soils. However, many of the roses that the northern gardener plants, such as the *rugosa* rose and Scotch rose, actually prefer lighter soils when on their own roots. The important point to remember is that roses must have a consistent supply of water and nutrients to grow to their potential. Virtually any type of soil can successfully grow roses if it is well drained and has enough organic content for good water retention and nutrient supply

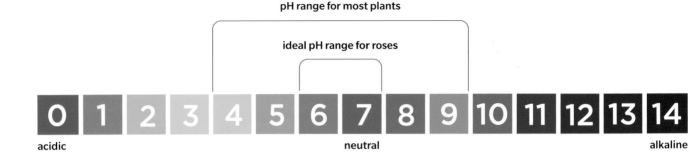

There are very few soils that require no work on the gardener's part to meet these conditions. Most of us live with soils that are not ideal. Your soil may be low in organic material, have a heavy clay texture that does not allow the free passage of air and water or may be so light soil that it will not hold water and dries out quickly. Your task as gardener is to improve those conditions. Depending upon your soil, this task can be simple or Herculean.

Acidity

One of the most important characteristics of soil is also one of the easiest conditions to alter. The soil of any site has a certain level of acidity or alkalinity. The level is measured using what is called a pH scale. The pH of a substance can range from 0 to 14, with 7 being neutral. Most plants grow in the 4 to 9 range. The ideal pH level for roses is 6 to 7. Within this range the rose can make best use of the elements available in the soil. If the soil has a low pH (acidic) or a high pH (alkaline), certain elements become chemically bonded to molecules and are unavailable to the plants. You can find out your soil's pH by having it tested.

If your soil is too acidic, add lime or gypsum to correct the problem. If it is too alkaline, add sulfur or iron sulfate to lower the pH. Your soil test should tell you the correct amount of these additives to bring your pH to the desired level. Most departments of agriculture will perform soil tests, or you can do these tests yourself using reasonably priced kits. Getting a soil test done is simple, yet it continually surprises me how few people take the time to do it. Without an accurate soil test, you are only guessing your soil's acidity level and playing roulette with your garden's health.

Texture

"Digging your hands into the earth" is a well-used phrase that deserves closer scrutiny. This phrase evokes images of seeds dropped into hoed trenches, roots settled into their new homes — in essence, the nurturing so central to good gardening. Yet this phrase concerns the texture of soil, and indeed, a soil's texture is of prime importance for good growth.

Most soils are composed of three basic textural materials — clay, sand and silt. The percentage of these major constituents plays a vital role in the texture of soil. Clay soils are often less well drained than other types of soil; however, as water passes through the clay it dissolves the surfaces of the mineral particles and provides vital elements to plants in the process. Clay soils contain a high percentage of minerals such as mica and feldspar. These minerals are made of tiny, flat plates that adhere closely together, making it difficult for water and air to penetrate between them. To break up clay, it is necessary to mix in large amounts of coarse-textured organic material. The odd-shaped chunks of organic matter hold the clay particles apart, creating spaces through which water and air can circulate.

Because most roots grow near the surface of the soil, it is best to work the majority of your organic material into this upper layer. Here the roots will benefit from the increased oxygen supply and the nutrients that the breakdown of the organic matter creates.

Sandy soils are quite different from clay soils. They drain well because they are composed of irregularly shaped particles of silica, eroded from quartz, which allow water and air to pass through the soil freely. Sand does not provide as much nutrition as clay because it does not dissolve easily in water nor contain as many minerals. The rapid passage of water tends to drain away the few nutrients available, and the soil can dry out quickly. The addition of organic matter can solve those problems. The organic material acts as a sponge that holds water, and the nutrients contained within the matter are gradually released as it is broken down by organisms in the soil. Indeed, some of the best soils in the world are composed of sand and organic matter. The combination of good drainage and the nutrient- and water-holding capacities of organic matter create excellent conditions for good growth. They are also far easier to work with than clay soils.

Silt is composed of fine particles — finer than sand but coarser than clay — derived from both water- and wind-borne erosion. Silt is generally very rich in minerals and drains relatively well. Some of the richest soils have a high proportion of silt; an old river system is a prime example of a place where you can find such soils. Most upland soils have a relatively small proportion of silt.

An easy way to test your soil for clay, sand and silt is to take a clear glass jar and add a good handful or two of soil. Fill the jar with water and shake it vigorously. Leave the soil particles to settle, and the three components of the soil will show as three distinct layers, with the sand at the bottom, the silt in the middle and the clay on the top.

Most garden soils lie somewhere between the extremes of clay and sand. In any case, the solution for improving your soil lies in the addition of organic material.

Organic material comes from the bodies of plants and animals. When broken down by the soil's microorganisms, the elements contained in them are released and combine with water percolating through the soil. This nutritious "soup" feeds your roses. If you examine the roots of a plant, note how the fine roots work their way through the pieces of organic material. They know where the soup is being served.

Two well-known sources of organic matter are manure and compost, which we will discuss in greater depth later. Another valuable soil conditioner available to most gardeners is peat moss. Its fine fibers have been chemically pickled by centuries of immersion in very acidic water. Although it contains few nutrients, it breaks down slowly and helps the soil hold both water and air effectively for many years. Shredded bark and other forest-industry by-products are also valuable. Sources such as leaves, grass clippings and prunings are thrown out by countless people, cities and businesses every day. Wise gardeners let it be known that they will accept any clean organic "waste." Properly composted, these wastes will add texture to your soil and will make digging your hands into the earth that much easier.

Mycorrhizae

One of the most exciting developments in soil science has been the discovery that plant roots do not act alone in the absorption of nutrients and water. Mycorrhizae are a type of fungi that forms a relationship with a plant, and this relationship benefits both the fungi and the plant. Most plants create recesses in the roots where the fungal threads of the mycorrhizae can attach.

Mycorrhizae both absorb water and break down organic matter in the soil. Because the mycorrhizal networks are often vast in size, the amount of water and nutrients made available to plants is many times that which could be absorbed directly by the roots. This not only gives a plant greater access to nutrients, but also a greater ability to survive drought conditions. In return the plants pump a portion of their sugars created by their leaves (as much as 25 percent) into the mycorrhizae.

One of the more staggering discoveries is that mycorrhizal networks in relatively undisturbed situations, such as in older forests, not only provide the trees with water and nutrients, but also distribute sugars from older trees to their seedlings growing underneath them, allowing them to survive even in the low light levels of the forest floor. When the older tree dies, these seedlings have a better chance of using the higher light levels provided by the death of the mother tree to grow quickly and occupy the space left open in the canopy.

Although few rose gardens will be located in old growth forests, the lesson is that the processes in a garden are the same. We should be very careful to disturb the soil as little as possible, so that mycorrhizal networks can establish and grow. Constant deep cultivation will interfere with this process.

Providing Nutrients

A healthy soil seethes with life. The soil's plants and animals go through countless cycles of birth and death. This produces waste products that, when dissolved in the soil's water, are the nutrients your rose uses for growth. Bacteria, and worm and insect manures are the primary sources of this nourishment.

To create more active soils you may have to kick-start your soil by adding organic supplements. These materials can be thought of as storehouses filled with the elements that were once used to construct the plants or animals that now make up these supplements.

Nitrogen is the key element involved in the breakdown process, and this starts at the microscopic level. If adequate levels of nitrogen are available, one-celled creatures such as bacteria

Underneath the mulch, the soil is home to many lifeforms, ▶
including earthworms that aerate soil and provide
nutrients.

begin to digest the fibers and other tissues in organic matter. Soon multicelled creatures consume bacteria, small insects consume these creatures and so on. As long as there is a steady addition of organic material, the process will continue. If no more organic matter is added, the nitrogen levels will increase until the existing organic material is consumed, then levels will slowly diminish. If large amounts of organic matter are added, the process will slow because there will be a temporary shortage of nitrogen for the bacteria. By maintaining a steady input of organic matter and nitrogen-rich materials, you can keep your soil humming with activity, a soil that can provide the nutrients your roses need to grow and flower well.

If you treat your soil as if it is simply a medium into which you introduce needed elements in the form of soluble fertilizers, you will gradually degrade your soil. Without sufficient organic material, the water-soluble elements in the fertilizers pass quickly through the soil. Your plant will absorb a certain amount of them, but most will leach out through the soil, ending up in the water table and eventually in the rivers. This excessive use of fertilizers has caused severe problems in lakes and rivers in many agricultural areas.

Although your plant will have absorbed some of the nitrogen, phosphorus and potassium from the synthetic fertilizer, these fertilizers often do not contain the numerous micronutrients that are also essential to proper plant growth. Micronutrients are those elements that are needed only in small quantities. They are, however, absolutely necessary. Without the tiny portions

of zinc, sulfur, selenium, boron and other such elements, the complex molecules that make up the plant's tissues cannot be constructed. It's like having the steel to build a bridge without the bolts to hold the pieces together. It is the organic material in your soil that contributes most of these micronutrients.

Another consideration when using synthetic fertilizers is their acidifying nature. As most fertilizers dissolve, they acidify the soil. For naturally acidic soils, it is essential that the pH be adjusted to compensate for this process. Many gardeners complain to me of not getting adequate growth, even though they are fertilizing heavily. When I ask whether they have added lime recently, their usual reaction is, "I didn't know it was necessary." By adding lime to their soil, they could use a fraction of the fertilizer and have much better growth.

Nitrogen is very important in the formation of the proteins necessary to build stems, leaves and roots. Other elements are important too, but nitrogen is more difficult to keep in the soil. It disperses into the air and is quickly leached away by rains. This instability creates a constant need to replenish nitrogen in the soil and makes it the focus of most fertilizer programs.

If you are committed to raising healthy, vigorous roses, you must be committed to building soil, for the former is dependent upon the latter. Though the soil's activities are complex, the practical solutions to fertilizing your rose beds are simple. Innumerable materials can be used to build better soils, but essentially we are talking about manures and composts.

The Magic of Manure

Most people would hardly consider manure a worthwhile topic of conversation. It is safe to say, however, that without the use of manure as a fertilizer, humans would still be hunter-gatherers. The conversion of human culture to an agricultural base required soils whose fertility could be sustained. The discovery of manure as fertilizer to increase crop yields and maintain soil texture made the Agricultural Revolution sustainable.

As food passes through an animal, its composition is altered. Fresh manure contains a high percentage of ammonia. This is partly why manure has such a pungent smell. Ammonia is high in nitrogen and is a readily available source for plants. As soon as the manure is exposed to the air, however, the ammonia begins to evaporate, and the nitrogen is lost to the atmosphere. As well, rain percolates through the manure, leaching out the nitrogen. So while fresh manure is a good source of nitrogen, older, exposed manure, although still valuable for its organic content, is not nearly as valuable as a fertilizer. A good farmer will work fresh manure quickly into the soil, so that the nitrogen will not be lost.

You should be cautious of fresh manure, however. It can contain high concentrations of ammonia, which may cause damage to plant tissues. Though ammonia in low concentrations provides nitrogen to plants, high levels of nitrogen can be destructive or even fatal. Fresh manure near a plant's roots provides a tremendous quantity of nitrogen, but as long as adequate water is available to the plant it will be able to handle the nitrogen. However, if water is limited in any way, the nitrogen will form salts in the plant's tissues, which will desiccate the plant from within. Manure also contains the bane of gardeners everywhere — weeds. Many weed seeds pass through animals without harm. Once put into the soil with the manure, they have not only a place to grow, but also the nutrition needed to grow well.

Because many gardeners today live in urban environments, the close connections between farmyard manure and the garden have essentially disappeared. Many gardeners may have only bagged manure available to them. Although often variable in quality and usually pricey, bagged manure is still a valuable soil enricher. It is also usually heat-treated to destroy weed seeds. The bagged manure may lack the nutrient value of a fresh pie from an alfalfa-fed Holstein cow, but it will still work magic.

No matter our source, if we want to use manure to best advantage we need to convert the nitrogen to a more stable form and to eliminate the problem of weed seeds. The answer is to make compost.

The Miracle of Compost

If you know how to make a complete, balanced compost, you do not need any other plant food. Well-made compost should contain all the nutrients needed for healthy growth. It will contain the bacteria, fungi and other microscopic life that work to control diseases in soil, and it will provide valuable organic matter.

The secret of good compost lies in balance. Bacteria in a compost pile feed on the carbon in the organic material and convert it into energy. The bacteria require nitrogen, phosphorus and potassium, among other elements, to accomplish this task. Although phosphorus and potassium are available in the organic material, nitrogen is usually in low supply. We need to add nitrogen to the pile. Fresh manure is the most common source of nitrogen for compost makers, but it is not always available. Many nitrogen-rich materials can be purchased at animal feed stores. These include alfalfa meal, linseed meal, soy meal, cottonseed meal, blood meal, bonemeal and feather meal. If you live near the sea you may be able to obtain fish or shellfish waste. Any of these, or similar high-protein materials, provide the nitrogen necessary to get your compost working.

A balance must be struck between the carbon and the nitrogen in the pile. The proper ratio for optimum compost activity is 40 carbon to one nitrogen. To achieve a healthy compost pile with a well-balanced carbon-nitrogen ratio, start as follows:

Spread your organic material into a layer approximately 1 ft. (0.25 m) thick. This might include materials like old hay, vegetable peelings, leaves (preferably shredded) or even weeds. On top of this, spread a layer of fresh manure approximately 3 in. (8 cm) thick. If you cannot obtain manure, scatter a heavy dusting of whatever organic nitrogen source you can obtain. If you are unable to obtain any organic sources of nitrogen, sprinkle a fertilizer such as urea (42-0-0) very lightly over your organic matter. Sprinkle a few shovelfuls of earth over the whole lot. This earth contains enough soil bacteria to act as a starter for the breakdown process, although many argue that it is not necessary. If you want a sweet (high pH) compost, add a dusting of lime, but because composts are naturally high pH, very little or no lime is needed. Repeat this layering until the pile is about 4 ft. (1.25 m) tall. As you

Compost is the result of decomposing plant material and contains a vast array of nutrients. It is the most valuable of soil amendments.

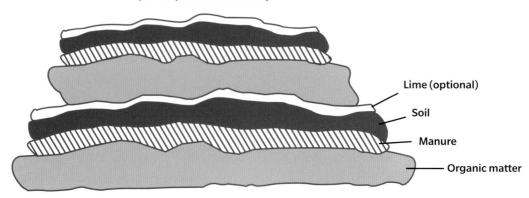

Taper the pile towards the top

Lime (optional)

Soil

Manure

Organic matter

Build your compost heap like a giant sandwich, layering nitrogen-rich materials between the bulk of organic materials. Keep the pile moist and turn often to introduce oxygen into the pile. The layer of lime should be a light sprinkling, with no depth. Too much lime will raise the pH to undesirable levels. The diagram above exaggerates the thickness of the soil and lime layers for illustration.

layer your pile, be sure to add enough water to make it thoroughly moist but not soggy.

Once your pile is built, turn it regularly. Turning a compost mixes the materials and, in the process, puts oxygen into the pile. Oxygen is vital to keep the important bacteria active. Some compost heaps never break down properly due to lack of oxygen. Turning every day or two is ideal, but few of us have that kind of time. If you can turn your pile once a week, or at the very least once every two weeks, the compost will still work well. After one or two turnings, your compost heap should be steaming hot inside. A properly balanced and aerated compost pile will reach temperatures of 160°F (72°C). These high temperatures destroy the weed seeds and any harmful diseases that may be present in the materials.

The size of your pile is not overly important; however, a small pile is better if kept confined by some sort of open-sided container that will keep the compost together while providing

oxygen for decomposition. If such compost piles have the proper carbon-nitrogen balance and if it is damp and turned regularly, it will work. Without some form of confinement, a small pile might have trouble developing the temperatures needed to break down the pathogens and weed seeds in the mixture. If space is limited or tidiness a concern, there are many compost makers available that are easy to use.

Once it cools, your compost is ready to use. The compost should look and feel like soil, although with a coarser texture. In the garden it will continue to break down, and as it does, will slowly release the nitrogen and other elements your plants need. If your quantities are limited, use it as a side dressing around your plants or incorporate some in your planting holes. If you have larger quantities, use it as a general top dressing on your garden. If you make composting a regular part of your garden program, you will see the results in healthy growth and good flowering.

Remember that incorporating it into the upper layer of the soil or under mulch so that it stays moist will give you the most benefit. A dry compost is not releasing nutrients efficiently. Be aware as well that compost is often as high as pH 8, so limit your addition of compost to no more than 25 percent of the soil's composition.

WEEDING

Ask a gardener what they like least about gardening and inevitably the answer is weeding. It is the subject books on gardening tend to avoid. After all, who wants to talk about work when you can talk about the scintillating colors, the exotic fragrances, the joys and beauties that gardening can create? But the truth is, a garden's beauty cannot unfold without weeding. Planting, watering, pruning, feeding and weeding are tasks that must be done, so that we can enjoy the results.

I enjoy weeding. After a hectic day I can think of no more relaxing activity than to go into my garden and weed. It allows me to be close to the plants, to touch them, to examine them for any problems, to enjoy them. Gardening for me, as it is for so many, is a spiritual exercise, and far from being repelled by weeding, I find it lends structure and discipline to the experience. At the same time, no one enjoys hacking at overgrown weeds, or working in gardens that resemble abandoned hay fields. The longer the weeding is neglected, the more work will be needed to bring the garden back under control. The secret to keeping weeds at a manageable stage is working with properly prepared ground and keeping to a regular schedule of maintenance.

Attitudes toward weeds vary from the relaxed to the compulsive. Whatever your attitude, keep in mind that weeds can teach us valuable lessons about our soil and our management techniques. Weeds are simply plants that are growing where we don't want them, but they are not a homogeneous group. Weeds differ in their habits and needs. By examining which weeds are growing in your garden, you can often discover whether your soil is too acidic or too alkaline, if cultivation is required, if the ground is lacking in certain nutrients and a host of other information. Turn weeding from a nuisance into an opportunity to learn more about your garden.

Weeding actually begins before you plant your first rose. If you are starting with a new piece of ground, the first order of business is to remove as many perennial weeds as possible, being sure to remove the roots to prevent the weed from regrowing. Although it is not exciting work, every hour you spend preparing your site will be repaid many times over in the future. Once the initial preparation is complete, you may want to add compost or manure. (Keep in mind that fresh manure will contain weed seeds.) Once you have planted your roses, seriously consider mulching with a layer of organic material such as shredded bark, leaves, grass clippings, straw or other materials that do not contain weed seeds.

Most seeds need light to germinate, so mulch will prevent light from reaching them. A layer of mulch will also keep many seeds from reaching the surface if they do germinate. Some will always manage to make it to sunlight, and any perennial roots that remain will send up shoots, but these are easily pulled in a mulched garden, an advantage that will be appreciated by those who have had to cultivate hard, baked ground,

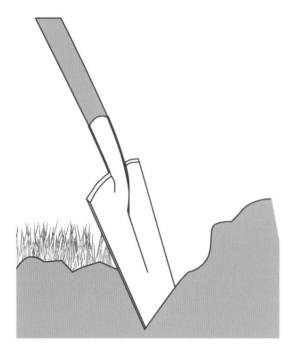

Edge your beds regularly. A steep vertical edge tends to discourage, at least temporarily, grass and weeds from growing into the bed.

from which the weed roots are nearly impossible to remove. A mulch keeps the ground looser and better aerated, making it easy to remove both the top and the root of the weed.

When planning your garden, remember that an isolated plant in a lawn is difficult to maintain. Grass moves in quickly. If you can plant in groupings or beds, you will be able to maintain the ground between the plants more easily. This makes lawn mowing much easier as well. Rather than having to push under a bush from all sides, the mower can simply follow the edge of the bed. This edge should be cut with a spade each spring to prevent grass or other weed roots from moving into the bed. Leave a cut face at the edge. This will tend to "air prune" any roots moving toward the bed. If your garden plan calls for individual plants on the lawn, keep the edge of the cultivated area

away from the plants. This will allow you to easily maintain that edge.

Weed Management

Weed new gardens often, particularly during the first few months. At this stage the weeds are not well established and are easy to deal with. If you wait, the roots will quickly spread, and pulling or hoeing will become increasingly difficult. Begin weeding early as well in established gardens. The spring and early summer are periods of intense growth. By getting to the weeding early, you will not have as big a job, and you will be able to relax during the summer when your roses are magnificent, and you are feeling warm and lazy.

Most weeding can be done in a mulched garden by simply pulling weeds out by hand. This requires only your hands and gloves, and perhaps the help of a three-pronged hand cultivator. If you prefer to keep your garden clean cultivated, there are several tools to aid you in your work. If you must choose only one tool to have, make it a hoe. This simple, age-old device has never been replaced as the number-one gardening aid. Several designs are on the market today, including hoes with triangular blades, push-pull types or ones with open U-shaped blades. The common hoe with a more or less rectangular blade is still the most popular design, although I am personally a big fan of the trapezoidal design called a "swoe."

Good hoeing is an acquired art. Most people hold a hoe horizontally and hack at the ground. This destroys both the hoe and your arms. A hoe should be held nearly vertically so

Hoe in a regular sequence of strips, always pulling undisturbed soil toward you as you proceed forward. Keep your hoe nearly vertical so that you slice rather than chop the soil.

works by interfering with the normal transfer of materials in the plant, killing the plant down to the root tips. Essentially these materials are labor replacers. Labor in agriculture is expensive, and using herbicides lowers expenses.

There is, however, a hidden cost to herbicides. Many of these materials work their way through the soil and into the groundwater, where they then show up in wells, rivers and ultimately the oceans. Areas treated with herbicides often cannot be planted with certain crops for years after the chemicals have been applied. Careless use of herbicides results in the loss of neighboring plants and contamination of soil and water. Children who play on lawns treated with herbicides can develop allergic reactions or illness. It is difficult to measure these hidden costs, but we need to carefully consider the consequences of using herbicides.

Herbicides are another unknown quantity in the chemical onslaught we are inflicting on Earth. Modern insecticides were introduced after World War II, and their use has accelerated at an alarming rate since. The harvest of that headlong rush into chemical management is now being reaped. Our water, air and soil are polluted. Plants, animals and humans are being affected in serious ways. Even our food is contaminated.

If we want to clean up our environment, we must make decisions that reflect that commitment. Herbicides are not needed in a garden, and I feel they have no place in gardening or agriculture. Any possible benefit we gain by their use is far outweighed by the consequences to ourselves, our children and all life on Earth.

the blade is at a proper angle to slice the earth, much like how a planer blade slices off shavings of wood. Try to slice off portions of soil no wider than half of the hoe's width. Work from left to right or vice versa, much as you might chew corn across the cob. Always walk forward, so you are slicing the earth ahead of you and pulling it back where you have already hoed. If you work moving backward you will be pulling soil and weeds over ground that has not been worked, making a good job nearly impossible. Such instructions may sound fussy, but you will be surprised at how much easier and productive hoeing is when done properly.

Weeds can be managed with the aid of chemicals. Called herbicides, these chemicals prevent weed seeds from germinating or destroy existing weeds. The newest generation of herbicides

PLANTING

When you purchase a rosebush, you hold in your hands the potential for many years of satisfaction and pleasure. To ensure that this potential is secure, you need to properly plant your rose. Roses can be planted any time the ground can be worked. Spring and fall plantings are somewhat less stressful on the plants, as the temperatures are cooler and there is often more rainfall. Roses planted in the summer will always be in containers. They must be watered regularly to prevent stress.

If you are planting a bare-root rose, the first order of business is to be sure that your rose does not dry out while you prepare the planting hole. As soon as you get your rose, plunge the roots in water for up to two hours. This will allow the plant to absorb as much water as it can hold. If you cannot plant it immediately, bury the roots in a trench in your garden or in damp bark or sawdust until you are ready. Remember that even a few minutes in a dry spot, especially in the sun, can mean disaster, as the fine hair roots, which are so important for water and nutrient uptake, will dry very quickly.

If the rose you purchase is a container-grown plant, be sure that any long, spiraling roots are teased out before you plant. If the roots have become a dense mass on the outside of the root ball and separating them is difficult, make several shallow cuts with a knife up and down the root ball. This will force the formation of smaller roots, which will grow into the new soil. Root-bound plants, if not unbound, will often not grow into the surrounding soil, and in the worst of cases can strangle themselves to death.

For container-grown roses, gently tease out the roots so they can grow naturally outward and better anchor the rose in the soil.

Root-bound plants are also easily pushed out of the ground by frost heave in northern areas.

When you prepare the planting hole, first remove any weeds, particularly their roots, from in and around the site. Dig a hole that is wide enough for the entire root system to spread out and deep enough so that the roots will be entirely underground.

Many roses are budded roses. Such roses have a bud of the cultivar inserted under the bark of a rootstock. A bulbous crook is formed at the union of the rootstock and cultivar. This union should be buried at least 4 in. (10 cm) below the soil surface. The soil will protect the union from the more severe winter temperatures and will help prevent suckering from the rootstock. Roses grown from cuttings or layers (also known as own-root roses) can be planted at the same depth as they were previously growing, or slightly deeper if you wish.

If you have a reasonably loose loam soil (soil that has a good balance of sand, silt and clay), mix in compost or well-rotted manure,

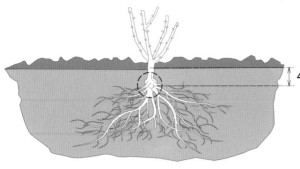

◄ When planting budded roses, be sure to bury the union 4 in. (10 cm) deep. This will protect the union from low winter temperatures, discourage rootstock suckering and encourage the cultivar to form its own roots.

4 in. (10 cm)

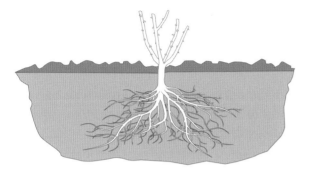

◄ Plant own-rooted roses at the same depth they were growing at before they were transplanted. Remember that the width of your planting hole is as important as the depth. Most feeding roots are shallow and will spread horizontally.

so that it constitutes 25 percent of the soil that will fill the hole. I also advise that you mix in a small handful of bonemeal and another of a high-protein meal such as blood, fish or alfalfa, as this gives the plant a long-term source of both phosphorus and nitrogen, which are needed for root and shoot development. If you wish to use peat moss, be sure that it is well moistened before you put it in the hole. Be careful not to have the peat moss account for more than one-quarter of the volume of the soil, as this may be too light a mix and may cause the hole to dry out quickly. This is especially important with heavier clay soils. These denser soils tend to draw water away from the lighter soil within the hole, so your rose will not receive adequate water in dry conditions. In wet weather the clay surrounding the looser soil in the hole will hold water, creating low oxygen conditions around the roots. If you have clay soil, it is usually best to use the

same soil you dug out of the hole, although amended with compost/manure and blood meal, fish meal or other high-protein meals. After the rose is planted, work in compost at the surface, where the feeder roots will form and will make best use of these nutrients.

As you plant the rose, be sure to work the soil around the root system so that no air pockets remain. These delay the formation of the smaller roots, which are so important in establishing your rose. Once you have worked the soil to the top, tamp firmly on the soil with your hands or feet. Leave a slight depression on the surface and fill this with water. Once it soaks in, fill the depression with water again until you are sure that the entire hole is completely saturated. If you are mulching, spread the mulch on the surface and give one more watering.

The most important part of establishing a new rose is watering. Keep a regular schedule of watering, giving the rose the equivalent of

While planting, handle the root ball gently so that it does not fall apart.

Once the rose is in place, tamp firmly on the soil around the root ball, and give the rose a good watering to settle the soil and eliminate air pockets.

at least 1 or 1.5 in. (2.5 or 4 cm) of rain a week. That is a fair amount of water. Be sure to soak the hole well. A few sprays on the surface will not do your rose any good. It takes more water than most people think to thoroughly soak down to the bottom of a planting hole. If there is sufficient rainfall you may not need to water, although be sure to check your soil, as sometimes rainfall will not penetrate very deeply.

If you are faithful about watering, your rose will repay you with good growth and more prolific blooming. Even a weak plant will thrive if given enough water. However, a plant can be overwatered, particularly in heavy clay soils. If the roots are kept too wet, they will lack sufficient oxygen. Common sense is your best guide in such situations.

MULCHING

I do not garden without mulches. A clean cultivated garden is an unnatural and often hostile environment for a plant. In hot, dry weather it becomes a desert. The soil at the surface absorbs and gives off immense quantities of heat and loses moisture rapidly. Rain can cause erosion, and the surface layer can become packed from the impact of raindrops. These impacts can also release fungal spores that are on the surface of the soil. After a rain, the sun can bake the muddy soil into a hard shell, reducing oxygen levels in the root zone and leading to even worse erosion problems in the next rainfall. In addition to all these factors, open soils are detrimental to mycorrhizal development.

Most plants prefer a "forest floor" type of environment. In a healthy forest the mulch layer is an equalizer. A mulch on your garden acts in the same way. Its insulating qualities temper the heat of summer and the cold of winter. Mulch absorbs and disperses the impact of falling raindrops, eliminating erosion and preventing soil bacteria and fungi from splashing up onto plants, where they can sometimes cause problems. The continual activity by worms, insects and other

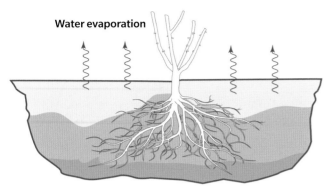

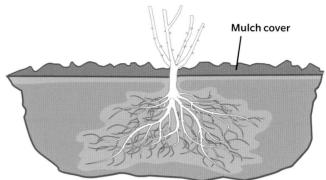

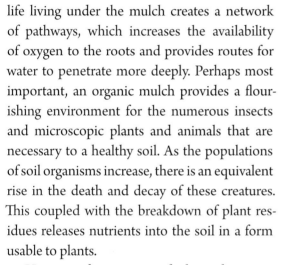

Water evaporation

Mulch cover

A clean, cultivated soil loses water rapidly in warm weather, and roots must penetrate deeply to obtain water.

Mulch cover on the soil reduces evaporation and helps create a wicking effect that keeps water levels evenly distributed throughout the soil. This allows the development of more fine-feeding roots near the surface, where soil activity is highest and nutrients most concentrated.

life living under the mulch creates a network of pathways, which increases the availability of oxygen to the roots and provides routes for water to penetrate more deeply. Perhaps most important, an organic mulch provides a flourishing environment for the numerous insects and microscopic plants and animals that are necessary to a healthy soil. As the populations of soil organisms increase, there is an equivalent rise in the death and decay of these creatures. This coupled with the breakdown of plant residues releases nutrients into the soil in a form usable to plants.

However, keep in mind that when you add a large amount of organic material to the soil, particularly high-carbon material such as wood chips and bark as you find in mulch, you increase the demand for nitrogen, which is needed by bacteria and other soil organisms to break down the carbon. Synthetic nitrogen fertilizers can provide this, although it does so at the expense of some of the soil's microscopic life because of the high acidity levels of these soluble forms of nitrogen.

A more sustainable approach is to incorporate a well-made compost into the surface soil just before adding your mulch. This will provide enough nitrogen and further improve your soil's texture and fertility. If the mulch layer is not worked into the soil, the nitrogen requirements will be fewer. Once this mulch stabilizes simply add new mulch on the surface every year or two, and the system will not overtax nitrogen supplies. This gradual layering mimics the annual addition of leaves to the forest floor.

In the garden you should not take away materials. With the exception of larger branches and such, try chopping up any stems, leaves and even weeds if they have not seeded. Spreading this material on the surface provides the very nutrients required by the plants, in turn reducing or eliminating the need for fertilizers. Why rake up all the leaves and other matter only to haul in composts, manures and mulches to replace the organic matter we have just collected and taken away? I call what we practice "messy gardening," although after a few weeks you will not be able to find the mess. Not everyone will ascribe to such a maintenance tool, but I urge you to try it.

Inorganic mulches such as solid plastic sheeting exclude oxygen from the soil and should not be used. Modern landscape fabrics allow passage of water and air, and will keep weed growth down for a while, but I have some major objections to them. They are a nightmare if you want to work your soil, and pulling them up after a few years in the ground can be a job to tax the patience of any gardener. Worst of all, they are created from nonrenewable petroleum products. It is bad enough that we squander these precious resources on such things, but to cover our gardens with them is not only unnecessary, but also unforgivable.

PRUNING

Pruning begins before you even buy your roses. It begins in your living room, when you are curled up in your easy chair deciding what rose to put in which space. The roses you choose all have distinctive growth patterns. If you have a space where you want a low-growing cultivar, don't put in a vigorous cultivar with the idea that you can keep it pruned down. Plant a rose that will best suit the space. If you don't, you will be constantly fighting against the natural growth pattern of the plant. You will create far more work than is necessary, and the results will never be as satisfying. Keep in mind that pruning is always a dwarfing process. To better understand what happens when you prune, it helps to visualize how a plant works.

Inside your rose, water and nutrients are absorbed by the roots and flow up the stems to the top of the plant. The leaves, harnessing the energy of sunlight, use the water and the carbon dioxide in the air to create sugars — a process known as photosynthesis. The sugars are sent throughout the upper portion of the plant, and any leftovers are sent down to feed the root system. Pruning removes potential leaf surface from your plant. Stems, to an extent, are also involved in the production of food. When you remove parts of the plant with your pruning shears, you are reducing a portion of this "food factory" and thereby limiting the plant's capacity for growth.

Pruning redirects growth in the plant. When portions of a plant are removed, it uses its remaining buds to form new stems and leaves. The food necessary to grow new parts comes, for the most part, from the root system, where much of the plant's food reserves are stored. If the root system is well established and has a good supply of food, the plant will be able to quickly replace the parts it has lost and even grow beyond that point. If a plant is weak and is severely pruned, it will take much more time to regain the capacity for growth it had before it was pruned. If the top growth cannot occur quickly enough to replace the food supply in the root system, the roots will starve and eventually the plant will die. It is essential, therefore, that pruning be kept to the minimum necessary to accomplish your purpose. Any more may needlessly weaken your plant.

However, don't be frightened into inaction, worried that you might harm your roses by pruning. Pruning is a useful art, allowing you to keep your roses in prime condition. By and large, the rose is a very forgiving and resilient plant.

Tools of the Trade

To do a good job of pruning, you have to have the right tools. This does not involve a major investment. Although the occasional 50-year-old *rugosa* rose may warrant a chainsaw, the only tools generally needed are the common hand-held pruning shears or secateurs and, for large old canes, a pair of long-handled lopping shears. Very large stems might require a pruning saw.

Pruning shears come in several designs and in a wide range of prices. If you are a serious gardener, spend a little extra. A precision-crafted pair of pruning shears that is kept sharp is a joy to use. A poorly made pair will cause nothing but aggravation, will not cut cleanly or easily and will probably have to be replaced far sooner than a well-built pair. There are two general types of shears. The anvil type has a flat surface with a central groove into which the blade descends. The bypass type act more like heavy duty scissors. The disadvantage of the anvil type is that the stem is crushed against the flat surface. The bypass type leaves a much cleaner cut and would certainly be the best choice for general pruning. The finest brands even come with replaceable parts. (Quality should govern your choice of all gardening equipment.)

Loppers are essentially shears with long handles, which gives a great mechanical advantage for pruning larger stems. Again, I would encourage you to purchase well-made bypass-type loppers, although there are anvil loppers with a ratchet action that can cut very large stems.

Another tool you may find useful is a small, pointed handheld pruning saw. With their thin, sharp blades, these are excellent for getting into

Using quality pruning tools will ensure good clean cuts, and you will avoid the frustration of working with inferior tools.

hard-to-prune areas or for removing branches that are too large for loppers. These saws can cut on either the pull stroke or the push stroke. For delicate work on smaller wood, a thin-bladed sharp knife is often the ideal tool. It is light, easy to maneuver and capable of smooth, clean cuts.

Last but definitely not least are gloves. Going into a rosebush without gloves borders on masochism. You can bet you're going to come out with blood on your hands, or worse, needle-thin prickles embedded in your skin; if these are not immediately removed, they will remind you of your foolishness for many days. The rose represents both the joy and the pain of love in literature. To a rose grower this metaphor needs no explanation.

Pruning a New Rose

A well-grown and well-handled young rose has a healthy root system endowed with numerous small, fine roots and several sturdy

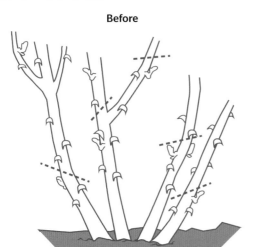

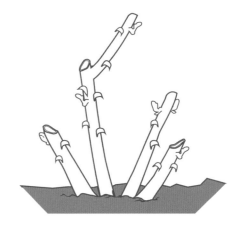

Pruning back a newly planted rose results in several stocky and vigorous shoots. Pruning to outside buds helps keep the center of the bush open.

stems filled with the food necessary for the season's growth. Such a rose, if planted in good soil and kept watered, should grow well and require only moderate pruning when planted. Unfortunately, some roses may have been underfed, grown under poor conditions, dug carelessly with a machine set at an improper digging depth or simply allowed to dry out somewhere along the often-tortuous route from the nursery to your garden.

The excitement you feel when your new roses arrive often fades when you open the package to find plants with a few dry roots and perhaps some mold growing where the tops were pruned. This scenario should be followed by emergency action. Soak the roots of such plants for at least two hours but not more than four hours. Cut off all dead wood and the stems to only a few buds. Because the roots will be very slow to absorb water, they will not be able to adequately supply it to all the emerging buds, and so the top will most likely wither, which is often followed by the death of the entire plant. By concentrating all its energies into a small area close to the root system, the plant can usually supply enough water and food to the remainder for vigorous growth. If your plant is a budded rose, be watchful for rootstock suckers and rub them off. If the rose is own rooted any new shoot will be welcome.

With luck your new roses will not be in such a sorry condition. For the average new rose a less rigorous pruning may do. However, as a general rule it is best to prune back a newly planted rose by 50 percent or so. By doing so you concentrate the growth in the remaining buds, which will tend to produce several strong shoots rather than many spindly ones.

When pruning your newly planted rose, make your cuts so that the last bud will grow outward. If you leave an inward-facing bud, you will often end up with crossed branches that will need to be pruned later. Make your cuts so that they slope slightly away from the bud. Cut fairly close to the bud, so that you will not end up with a dead stub, which can become infected with canker, but not so close that the bud will be in danger of drying out. An eighth of an inch (3 mm) is about the right length.

Examine the roots before planting and prune off any dead ones. If the ends of any roots are ragged or torn, prune them off cleanly. Do not prune any more than necessary from the root system. The more roots available to the plant, the more water and nutrients it will be able to absorb and the quicker it will be able to recover from transplanting. The exception to this is when you are transferring to a pot. Here the roots should be pruned to fit comfortably into the pot without having to be bent.

Please note that if you are planting a rose that does not repeat bloom, such as *alba* and *gallica* roses, you should be more sparing when you prune, as such roses will only bloom off the last year's growth. A hard pruning would eliminate most of the wood, and you may not get any bloom the first year. Hopefully, your plant will be vibrant and healthy and not require drastic pruning.

Maintenance Pruning

Once your new rose has established itself, a program of maintenance can begin. The question of when to prune has always been a source of debate. Successful pruning can be accomplished in spring, summer or fall depending on your purpose.

Spring pruning will result in very vigorous vegetative growth. Early summer or midsummer pruning is useful for creating smaller stems that will result in a denser plant. Pruning in late summer may initiate soft late growth, which may not withstand hard frost and will be more susceptible to winter kill. Fall pruning should be done when the plant is going into dormancy.

Wait until the leaves turn color and start to fall. The longer you wait, the more food will be delivered to the root system, and the more vigorous your rose will be the following spring.

Most growers still prefer early spring for their pruning, and I think a good case can be made for delaying pruning until spring in the northern garden. Many of the roses we grow in the north will kill back a certain percentage each winter. If you wait until spring to prune, it will be easier to assess the amount of damage that the plant has suffered, and the plant can be pruned accordingly. The dead portions can be removed and the remainder shaped. However, spring can often be a very busy time for gardeners. If you know that your time will be at a premium in the spring, by all means prune in the fall. The hardier cultivars will probably not suffer; just leave the more tender types until spring.

When you begin pruning, first take out dead or diseased portions and remove any crossed branches. If your rose has already grown larger than you wish, remove older stems and weaker thin wood and cut back the top to the desired height. When thinning out branches within the plant, cut back to the next branch. This will create a more natural appearance and will avoid numerous stubs, which give the plant a butchered look and invite disease. The top branches should be cut so that an equal space is given to each branch. Cut to a bud that will grow into the empty spaces. As the shrub types age, it is advisable to cut out the oldest canes. This will continually rejuvenate the bush, leaving younger, more floriferous wood

Keep your hedge widest at the base so the the entire leaf surface receives adequate light.

and helping to keep the plant within reasonable limits.

Many people feel incompetent when it comes to pruning. It is perhaps the most mysterious and least understood of horticultural endeavors. Indeed, the sorry results of unsympathetic pruning can be viewed on any street. Conversely, the result of neglecting pruning can be an overgrown tangle. If you are unsure of how to begin, try stepping back from your subject. Think how your plant should look. Is your rose a vigorous, rounded shrub? Is it a tall, wiry climber? Visualize the perfect plant (of the kind you are dealing with) and superimpose it on your specimen. Pick out and retain the main structural elements. Eliminate the growth that is superfluous to the shape you desire or that extends beyond the limits you want to impose on it. If you can work with the natural growth pattern of your subject, you will be able to achieve a harmonious result. If you are constantly fighting against the plant's growth pattern, the results will look stilted. As with so many things in life, experience is the best teacher. The more pruning you do, the more confident you will become.

Pruning Hedges

The first few years are critical when developing hedges. Once you have decided upon the general shape of your hedge, remove the growth that is beyond the imaginary planes of the hedge's sides and top. As the plants continue to grow, your spring pruning will be removing more material each year. It may also be desirable to prune after the first flush of flowering to remove wayward branches. Always be sure to keep the base of the hedge wider than the top, so that adequate light is available to the entire surface of the hedge. If you try to maintain a vertically sided hedge, or if you try to curve the lower edge to form a ball shape, the bottom section will not receive enough light and will become open with only the branches showing.

As the hedge ages, you should systematically remove the oldest canes in the plants. Removing a few stems each year will not create large and noticeable holes and will encourage new and more productive wood to form. Your hedge will flower better, and you will be creating enough space for light and air to reach the inner parts of the hedge.

Roses lend themselves to an informal style of hedge. Although it is possible to create a more formal geometric style with careful attention to pruning, the continual shearing needed to maintain the sharp edges of such a hedge tends to form a rather dense outer "skin," which does not allow good light and air penetration into the interior of the hedge. By pruning too often you will destroy many of the developing flower buds, and your hedge will not be as colorful. If you desire a formal hedge, it is probably advisable to stick with plants that lend themselves better to this use.

If you have a sunny area where an informal hedge would be effective, roses can be a choice hedging material. With gentle shaping and careful renewal, you can maintain a wall of color that will be useful and visually exciting.

Pruning Older Roses

Among the hardy roses, many will form good-sized shrubs. They are vigorous, permanent elements in the landscape and will endure for decades. As they mature they gradually thicken, often becoming very dense. This can result in plants that are really empty shells. The center of the bush receives very little light. As a result, no growth occurs on the inside, and only the tips of the outer branches, which have access to sunlight, will put on new growth.

With many vigorous roses such as the *Rosa rugosa* selections and hybrids, an overgrown plant can be dealt with firmly. We have often taken 5 to 6 ft. (1.5 to 1.75 m) plants and cut them back to 18 in. (46 cm) in the early spring. Once the new height is established, we remove the oldest canes and thin the remainder. The tips are pruned to a bud that faces in the desired direction, and any suckers are removed

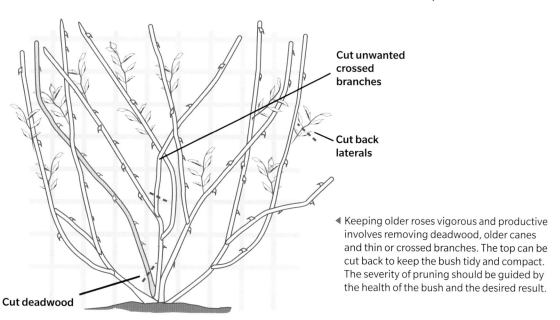

Cut unwanted crossed branches

Cut back laterals

Cut deadwood

◀ Keeping older roses vigorous and productive involves removing deadwood, older canes and thin or crossed branches. The top can be cut back to keep the bush tidy and compact. The severity of pruning should be guided by the health of the bush and the desired result.

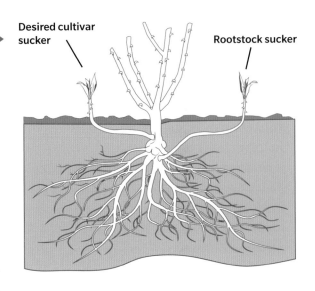

Suckers produced by the rootstock should be removed ▶
immediately, for they divert growth from the desired
cultivar, and they will not produce the desired flowers.
Suckers from the desired cultivar can be removed or left,
depending on how far you want your rose to spread.

Desired cultivar sucker

Rootstock sucker

from the perimeter. At first the plant looks a bit butchered, but within a month or so the new growth fills in and the plant looks better than ever. This is admittedly drastic action, but as long as the plant is healthy, there will be no detrimental effects.

Ideally, pruning is an ongoing process, which begins when the plant is young and continues annually. If you are attentive to removing a few of the oldest canes each year to open the inside of the plant to light and trimming back the sides and top to your desired height, you can keep your rose healthy and floriferous without resorting to the medieval treatment mentioned above.

There may be times when a rose is so overgrown that the best option is to simply remove the plant and plant a new one, or to keep a section of the plant and treat it as a new plant. Whatever method you choose, gloves and a great deal of determination are vital.

It should be noted that some species such as *Rosa foetida* and its hybrids resent hard pruning. A light and regular touch is needed when dealing with such roses.

Suckering Problems

Many roses are prone to suckering. They are, after all, briars and use suckers to grow outward and to replace older, less productive wood. Suckers are more accurately called "underground stolons," and they are specialized stems. Suckers appearing on budded roses are often misunderstood by the new rose

grower. When long vigorous shoots appear they believe their rose is doing well and leave the shoots to grow. But once the suckers begin blooming, they are disappointed and tell me their rose "has gone wild."

A rose can be either on its own roots or budded (grafted) onto a rootstock. If your rose is on its own roots any suckers that occur from below the ground will have the same flowers and growth habits. The vigorous shoots that grow from the base of an own-rooted plant will branch and be the source of many new flowers.

If your rose is budded, the suckers that grow from below the bud union will be quite different from the rose grafted on top. It is essential that these suckers be removed as soon as they are noticed. They should be pruned off at the point from where they are growing out of the main stem. If a stub is left, it will usually grow several new shoots from the remaining buds. If pruning with shears is difficult, the shoot can be pressed down at the base until it breaks off the main stem. The injury to the stem can result in infection with crown gall or other diseases, but in actuality it rarely harms the plant and is often the most effective way to deal with suckers. Burying the bud union well below the surface will go a long way toward lessening the incidence of suckering.

Hard pruning and winter injury can often stimulate sucker production. This is not a problem for an own-rooted rose, but it is with a budded rose. For me, it is a good argument to purchase and grow own-rooted roses.

Further Maintenance

A few pruning techniques can be used with good effect during the growing season. When a cluster of flowers has finished blooming, the section of the stem just below the flowers does not grow any more. New growth starts from the first vegetative bud below the flower cluster, but if the plant's energy is diverted to the formation of seeds, that bud will be inhibited from growing. If the old cluster is pruned off immediately following flowering, then any possible seed is removed. The plant's hormonal balance will instead shift toward the production of more growth, so it can flower and produce seeds elsewhere. Sugars will be delivered to the new growth point, and the waiting bud will be stimulated to grow. Within a few weeks, you will have another bloom. This is only effective on repeating roses. And obviously, if you want rose hips you won't want to practice this technique. Single-bloom cultivars can be deadheaded or not, depending on whether you desire rose hips.

Some roses leave their petals in a messy, brown lump when they have finished blooming.

Deadheading balled or finished flowers on repeat- ▶
blooming roses will result in speedier rebloom.

Some may also "ball," a term that refers to when water saturates the outside petals of a bud, and when they dry the bud cannot properly open. The removal of spent or balled blooms will help to maintain a fresh look to the plant and, for the reasons mentioned above, will encourage new growth.

Be on the lookout for problems such as rose galls. These swellings are formed by small wasps that lay their eggs in the stems. Upon hatching, the larvae feed on the inside of the stem, causing it to swell and in the process killing the growth above the swelling. If allowed to complete their life cycles they will infect other roses. Cut out any unnatural swellings as soon as they are noticed. Various infections such as cankers should also be cut out as soon as you notice them. These often start on dead wood such as pruning stubs or winter-injured branches. They can quickly work their way into live tissue and cause a great deal of damage if not tended. You can read more about dealing with these and various other pests and diseases in the next chapter.

4 INSECTS AND DISEASES

From above, a casual observer sees a garden murmuring with wind through long-stemmed grasses and fragrant with newly opening roses. But between sand particles, inside last year's decaying stems and on the surfaces of countless leaves and branches, a frenetic drama is taking place with all the cycles of life and death being played out in fantastically intricate patterns.

It is understandable that many people recoil from insect life. Its forms are so bizarre to us, its patterns so seemingly unrelated to our own. Yet the interested observer who takes the time to gain a better understanding of the insects' life cycles and how they interact in the garden will soon not only develop a fascination for them, but will also better appreciate how important the diversity of insect life is to the health of our gardens and ultimately our planet.

◄ We are not the only creatures that love roses. They are food for many species, like the thrips that attacked this rose.

Not all arthropods are unwelcome in the garden. Spiders and other predators keep pest populations down.

There are a number of insects whose lifetime ambition is to suck or chew on rosebushes, so that they can obtain all the vitamins, minerals and other necessities needed to produce a new generation to carry on their species. You, the gardener, want to keep your roses healthy, so that you can enjoy the sensual splendors they provide. You will need to make some important decisions.

The average manual on roses contains a formidable list of chemical insecticides. Let's take a closer look at what happens to the ecology of a garden when insecticides are used.

Most insecticides kill a wide spectrum of insect species, usually by affecting their nervous or digestive systems. These kill not only insects inhabiting the leaves and branches of the bush, but also other insects and soil microbes when the chemicals wash into the soil. These other creatures may be playing important roles in keeping your garden healthy. As rain and sun wash away and degrade the insecticide residues, insect life returns to the sprayed areas. However, with the numbers of many insects reduced, the new balance is quite different.

Every insect has a predator. Without such predators, we would be scraping aphids off our cars in the morning. When we spray our roses we kill not only the pests we want to be rid of, but their predators as well. When the surviving pests, or those arriving from other places, start to reinfest the rosebush, few predators remain to keep them under control. This often results in devastatingly high populations of pests, which, if not sprayed again, will do serious damage to your plants. Predators always reproduce more slowly than their food source, otherwise the predators would rapidly eat up their food source and die. In other words, there must always be a population of food (the pests we want to be rid of) present to maintain predator populations. The key to biological control of pests is to be able to maintain high enough populations of predators to keep pests from doing unacceptable damage to your plants.

When you spray insects with an insecticide, most of them will die, but not all. Every creature on Earth is unique, with its own set of characteristics, its own genetic code. So while most insects in a population will be killed by a particular poison, certain individuals may be tolerant to it. If they survive to reproduce, they pass on their tolerance to the new generation. After many generations, entire populations of insects may become tolerant to certain insecticides. This phenomenon is well documented and has caused much concern in conventional agricultural circles. For several years our nursery sprayed its plants with insecticidal soap. This substance is relatively nontoxic to mammals, but is effective against many soft-bodied insect species, like aphids. We noticed after several years that we seemed to need more and more soap to control our aphid populations. It took a while for the truth to sink in. We were creating a race of aphids that could tolerate soap. We had, in effect, outsmarted ourselves. Genetic diversity had triumphed. It was this fact, together with the realization that an annual spray program locked us into a spray-or-die cycle, that convinced us to reexamine our insect control program.

If you wish to adopt a nonchemical approach to gardening, you must first realize that insects are an important part of the garden. Just because it crawls or flies, an insect is not necessarily an unwanted alien. Nearly all insects in your garden are benign or actually helpful by keeping other insect populations in check, by pollinating your flowers, by aerating the soil or by performing any number of countless tasks that keep the garden healthy. There will always be some unwanted insects that will feed on your roses. If we are to make a serious commitment to eliminating harmful chemicals from our gardens and our agricultural community, we must change our zero-tolerance approach toward insects. We must accept a certain amount of damage as nature's due. But if you recruit your allies, this damage can be kept inconsequential.

The health of your plant is of paramount importance in reducing insect problems. A

The larval stages of many insects can do a great deal of damage to leaves, buds and flowers.

healthy plant reflects a healthy soil and a proper site. If you have looked after the basic requirements of your rose, you will have far fewer problems. An actively growing plant is less subject to insect injury. There is a growing body of evidence that plants under stress are more attractive to insects. They are less efficient at producing the compounds that deter pests. It makes perfect sense that a well-fed plant is more likely to remain healthy. Good parents feed their children well, so that they do not suffer from disease. So it should be with our garden charges.

Another fascinating line of research has shown that, when attacked by an insect or disease, plants emit chemicals into the air, and possibly sounds, that warn others of its species of an impending infestation. When the plants pick up on these warnings, they begin producing molecules that repel the invaders. What used to sound like hocus-pocus science fiction turns out to be true.

Gardeners constantly seek out plants with beautiful flowers, unusual color, good vigor and pleasing form. The gardener who is committed to reducing the use of chemicals should pay strict attention to those that exhibit good resistance to insects and diseases. Roses differ dramatically in their tolerance to insects. When choosing cultivars, select those that will make your job easier. It is encouraging that disease and insect resistance are now becoming important criteria for judging new roses, a trend that is both welcome and long overdue.

As we sit in our gardens enjoying the pleasures they bring, we often revel in the companionship of birds. Whether calling out their melodious songs or enchanting us with their multicolored plumage, they add a charm to a garden that few fail to appreciate. But birds are much more than colorful ornaments. They are important insect predators and consume nearly their own weight in food every day. This can have a tremendous impact on a garden. By supplying shrubs, trees and perennials that provide food, nesting sites and perches, you can enlist one of the most effective means of pest control.

Diversity in a garden is a tremendous asset. Most insects go through several phases during their lifetime. By offering an assortment of plants, you can provide sites for predators to complete their life cycles. As an example, in the fall our grapevines harbor clusters of ladybugs, which often number in the hundreds. Ladybugs prey on aphids. Although we do not know why the ladybugs are there (they do not harm the vines), they use the shelter of the grape leaves to gather and perhaps mate. There

are countless similar examples. A healthy garden is a diverse garden.

Last, never underestimate your power as a predator. Often an infestation of insects can be easily controlled by simply going into your roses and picking off the culprits. Some small sucking insects can be washed off your roses with a strong spray of water. Once on the ground they are easy prey to the insects that patrol the soil surface. If you know your roses' enemies, you can be a deadly predator.

COMMON INSECT PESTS OF ROSES

If you choose to use biological methods against insects, a better understanding of insect pests is your best weapon. This section contains information on some of the more common pests of roses in northern areas. By learning about the life cycles of these insects, you may discover ways you can interfere with cycles and prevent large populations from building up in your garden. There is no doubt that we can learn from listening to the advice of experts, but remember that anyone with the ability to observe can find new solutions to old problems.

Aphids (*Aphis* spp.)

Aphids are perhaps the most common pest of roses. They are small, soft-bodied, lime green or brown creatures that puncture a plant's soft new-growing tissues with their mouth parts and draw in its juices. Severe infestations will cause the young leaves to curl and dry up. Aphids are nearly always found on the undersides of the leaves, near the tips of the shoots.

The growing tips are where growth is rapid, and the plant is pushing its sugar-rich sap. It's also where their tiny feeding tubes can easily penetrate. As the aphids feed, they excrete a sticky residue that is attractive to ants. Certain types of ants feed on this "honeydew" and will even protect an aphid colony from other insects. If there is a great deal of honeydew, it will often appear blackish on the stem's surface, as molds and fungi begin to grow on it.

Aphids are one of the most prolific insects in existence and also have one of the most amazing life cycles. They overwinter as tiny blackish eggs on the stems, usually near a bud. In the spring small nymphs hatch from the eggs and quickly grow to full size. These first aphids are called stem mothers. They have the unusual ability to hatch their live young without fertilization from a male. Several generations are produced in this manner. Then a generation is born with wings. These winged aphids, called migrants, fly to other plants, some to the same species of plant, others to a summer host

plant — usually an annual of some kind. These aphids continue to produce generations of unfertilized young throughout the summer. As the days grow shorter a generation is produced that contains both winged females and winged males. The females, called fall migrants, fly to the kind of plant on which they started in the spring, then give live birth to wingless females, which must be fertilized by the males to produce eggs. The eggs are laid around the buds and crevices of the plant. In the spring these hatch out, and the cycle is repeated.

Each aphid is theoretically capable of producing millions of aphids by the end of its cycle. The reason we are not swimming in aphids is because so many other insects and birds consume aphids. Early in the spring small solitary spiders can be observed catching and eating aphids. Soon predators such as the small gall midge and the larvae of the syrphid fly begin feeding on them. As spring progresses, the most efficient enemy of the aphid appears. When aphids begin to multiply, adult ladybugs arrive at the aphid colonies and lay their eggs. After about two weeks, tiny, opaque and ravenous larvae hatch and begin feeding. They hold the aphids upside down in their large mandibles and suck their insides out. In only a few days these larvae grow to nearly 20 times their original size and eliminate the colony of aphids. They move from colony to colony until they reach full size. They then form a hardened shell and pupate. In two weeks or so they emerge as the winged ladybugs that most everyone recognizes. They are rounded beetles, usually red or yellow with several dark spots on their wings. Although ladybugs eat some aphids at this stage, it is their young that are every aphid's nightmare.

It is imperative that you do nothing when aphids first appear on your roses. Spraying at this stage, even with soap or similar nontoxic substances, is a tragic mistake, for the ladybug's eggs or larvae, as well as other predators, will be killed. You must grit your teeth and bear them for a while. After two weeks or so you should begin to see the small ladybug larvae at work and will notice colonies of aphids reduced to empty white husks. Once the ladybugs establish a presence, the aphids will be kept to minimal levels. If your roses are growing in a light sandy soil, you may find that ants are protecting aphids from predators. This can be alleviated by spreading a layer of mulch in the garden. Ants prefer dry, well-drained conditions; under a mulch there is a great deal of moisture, and the ants will not be encouraged to build their colonies.

If you are raising roses in a greenhouse, where ladybugs cannot enter, you have several options. It is possible to buy predators from companies that specialize in biological controls. Another simple but effective control is to hose plants down regularly with a well-directed and strong stream of water. Insecticidal soap can also be effective against aphids, and may be necessary in the greenhouse, where normal insect relationships are disrupted.

Roses vary tremendously in their attractiveness to aphids. One hardy old favorite, F.J. Grootendorst, is notorious as a gourmet treat for aphids. At the nursery we used to spray this cultivar often to try to keep the aphid population down, with only limited success. Once we let the predators do our work, we found that, after the required waiting period, our Grootendorsts become a wonderful place to study predators in action. Now our Grootendorsts stay relatively clean all season. In contrast, a newer cultivar, Champlain, must be last on the aphid's list of restaurants, because we never see the pests on this rose.

Gall Wasps (*Diplolepis* spp.)

Gall wasps are tiny insects, usually black or orange in color. They are so small that a hand lens is necessary to see them well, and they are usually noticed only when a gall forms on the rose, around the larval stage. The galls interfere

Tiny but terrible, the gall wasp destroys all growth above the swellings that form around its eggs.

with the flow of water and nutrients to the sections of stems above them, and occasionally large numbers of galls are noticeable. The growth is caused by the reaction of the plant to the infestation, and the results are swelling or other often curious growths. Where no control is practiced, infestations can build up to levels that can seriously reduce the vigor of your roses.

There are several species of gall wasps. One causes a moss-like gall called Robin's pincushion, moss gall or rose bedeguar gall. These are rather fantastical looking, like a tuft of soft yellow and reddish fibers. Others produce small light red round hollow chambers with small dark red spines. The gall that is most concerning, however, is the species that produces a swelling on the stem, usually near its base.

In the spring, adult wasps lay their eggs in the stem of the rose. These eggs hatch in approximately four days. Once the larvae begin feeding, the plant reacts by producing masses of tissue around the larvae. The larvae overwinter in these protective galls. In spring they pupate. When their host plants are at the proper stage, the adult wasps eat holes through the sides of the galls, emerge and lay their eggs to begin the new generation.

All growth above the gall will die. The appearance of a dying stem in the middle of a healthy bush is a sign of gall wasp activity. Follow the dead stem down to near the ground and you will find the gall. If immediate action is taken the damage can be limited. Remove the gall and burn or bury it.

Insects like the Japanese beetle are exceptionally voracious, and aggressive methods should be used to keep their population under control.

Japanese Beetles (*Popillia japonica*)

Although this rapacious pest is limited somewhat by severe winter temperatures, it is very active in warmer areas to Zone 5. Recently, they have been found in cooler zones, where formerly it was not believed they could survive. This is an apparent example of natural selection at work, aided by the increased movement of pests as hitchhikers on human cargo and Earth's rising temperatures. All together it means we will see more Japanese beetles in the future.

These are stunning beetles with gleaming green and gold wings. They are also stunning in their capacity to chew through any number of different plants. One of their favorites is the rose.

Japanese beetles prefer to spend their larval and pupal stages in the soil underneath sod. This fact has made our suburban lawns fertile ground for hatching new beetles. An older method of eradicating the beetles involved spreading a powder that contains bacteria called milky spore on the lawn. The spores filter down into the soil, where the larvae are wintering. If the larvae ingest the spores they will be paralyzed and die. The bacteria then spread throughout the soil, and in a few years most larvae will not survive in the treated area.

A newer treatment involves releasing nematodes (*Steinernema* spp.) into the soil. These are tiny worm-shaped creatures that travel through the soil searching out larval and pupal hosts, which include the Japanese beetle and many other grub species such as June bug (June beetle) and sod webworm. This solution works quickly. The nematodes are sprinkled on the affected lawn. They need moisture, so the spreading should be done in the rain or followed immediately by a good soaking. Once in the moist soil the nematodes search out a larva and enter it through its bodily openings. They release bacteria that kills the larva within two days. Nematode eggs are laid inside the body, and the newly hatched nematodes feed on the larva, then leave to find new hosts. Different species of *Steinernema* nematodes can be used to control different types of larvae. Be sure the species you use is recommended for Japanese beetles. Most garden centers will be familiar with this issue, and you can always check the Internet.

Rose Chafers
(*Macrodactylus subspinosus*)

This is a small greenish to tan beetle with orange-brown legs. The adult phase flies and

The rose chafer can be a nuisance in some gardens, while other gardens may rarely see it.

they feed on a number of plants, including fruit trees and grapevines, but they love to feed on rosebuds. There is a single generation per year. After feeding for several weeks the female adult lays her eggs in a grassy area, usually in a sandy soil. The hatching eggs feed on the roots of grasses and other plants. They eventually burrow down before winter and pupate. The adults emerge in late May or early June.

This pest is more prevalent in areas with sandy soil. If small numbers of adults are present they can be caught and destroyed. If numbers are high you can purchase sticky traps with a floral-scented lure that attracts the adults. These traps attract Japanese beetles as well. We recommend that you place the traps well away from your roses, so the beetles are not attracted to your plants.

Similar to dealing with Japanese beetles, you can release nematodes (*Steinernema* spp.) into the soil, where they will destroy the overwintering larvae.

Rose Midges
(*Dasineura rhodophaga*)

This small yellowish fly lays its eggs deep within the sepals of a rose's buds. Sepals are the green modified leaf structures that surround the petals. Once the eggs hatch the tiny larvae feed on the expanding bud, distorting or killing the bud before it opens. The larvae then descend to the ground, where they pupate and emerge the following spring as adults.

A large infestation can mean few flowers. A simple and effective method is to pluck off and destroy any buds that show symptoms. The attentive gardener can put a quick end to that generation of midges. Because the larval stage overwinters just below the surface of the soil or in the mulch under its plant host, some place a goodly layer of mulch around the plant in fall or remove any existing mulch and replace it with new mulch.

Similar to dealing with Japanese beetles and rose chafers, you can release nematodes (*Steinernema* spp.) into moist soil or mulch under the affected plants.

Spittlebugs (*Hemiptera* spp.)

Spittlebugs are also known as froghoppers. They are usually noticeable only when they surround themselves with a protective layer of white foam, which looks like spit. They have sucking mouthparts that draw sap from the stems of many plants, including roses.

They begin life as eggs laid on a host plant. The eggs hatch into small green nymphs. During the year they molt, gaining size as they

Rose midge damage is disheartening, but destroying affected buds will help to reduce populations.

The spittle bug is a curious but relatively harmless pest on roses.

do so. Eventually, they mate and lay eggs in the fall for next year's generation.

Although noticeable, spittlebugs do little harm to roses. Occasionally, a larger than normal number may appear on bushes, but these can be easily sprayed off with a garden hose or picked off by hand. I find them interesting and inoffensive, and rarely take the time to destroy them.

Other Pests

Patrol your roses and learn to recognize the presence of such pests. Usually, hand picking will take care of an infestation if caught early. The earwig, a nocturnal species, can be caught in traps made of strips of corrugated cardboard. They crawl into the corrugation at daybreak and can then be disposed of in a pail of soapy water. Solutions to pest problems are often simple. Both an expert and your neighbor may have answers. Magazines, gardening books and the Internet are mines of information. And remember, if you look with open eyes you may find your own solutions.

DISEASES OF ROSES

Roses have a reputation as troublesome plants that need to be constantly coated with various fungicides to prevent the diseases to which they are prone. In part, this reputation is deserved. Many roses, particularly in more humid climates, fall victim to rusts, mildews and that most ubiquitous of rose diseases, blackspot. The modern hybrid teas and floribundas are quite susceptible to fungal diseases, although breeders are now producing healthier cultivars. The popularity of the hybrid teas, coupled with this weakness, has helped to give the rose its reputation as a difficult subject. The northern rose grower should take heart. A good percentage of hardy roses are bred from healthier species. With careful planning, you can choose roses that will require little, if any, protection from diseases. At the same time, there are hardy roses that, though prone to some diseases, are so lovely that we cannot bring ourselves to garden without them. So a little advice is in order.

In general, fungi, which are among the more serious diseases, are spread in damp conditions. While it is impossible for you to change the weather, you can help discourage fungi. The placement of roses is so important. If your roses are placed within a garden where there is very little air movement, they will take much longer to dry after a rain and will tend to hold the humidity around them. Roses placed where there is good air movement will dry out more quickly and will, therefore, have drier foliage. This will often make the difference between a heavy infestation, a light occurrence or even total absence of disease. Sunlight helps to inhibit fungal growth, and the availability of sun is of great importance in preventing it. Pruning roses to open up the bush will increase both air movement and sunshine within the bush.

Rose cultivars differ dramatically in their resistance, or lack of resistance, to disease. If you want to stay away from fungicides, you would be well advised to choose cultivars with disease resistance in mind. The descriptions and lists at the back of this book will aid you in your choice.

Be sure to remove any material pruned from roses suffering from disease. Also be observant and careful when pruning. Branches and stubs left by careless pruning techniques often give diseases like cankers a place to take hold. From there they can move into living tissue, where they can cause severe damage.

Blackspot (*Diplocarpon rosae*)

Without a doubt, blackspot is the most common scourge of roses. Most roses are at least partially susceptible, and some cultivars can become defoliated if it is not controlled. As its name suggests, the symptoms are black or brown spots, which begin to appear in early summer. The previous year's infected leaves release millions of spores into the air, which settle on the leaves and begin to grow. Blackspot generally shows up first on the older, lower leaves and can eventually infect the entire shrub.

It is helpful to remove and burn or compost any infected foliage on or under any disease-prone bushes. This will reduce the number of spores the next season. A new layer of mulch each fall will bury overwintering spores and prevent them from dispersing. Keep susceptible cultivars pruned to an open shape and try to get as much air movement as possible around the plants. Peter Beales, in his book *Classic Roses*, recommends using overhead sprinklers every 10 days at night for periods of at least five hours as a preventive measure. The continual washing removes many of the spores from the leaf surface. Although I have not tried this personally, it may be worthwhile.

If you wish to grow some of the more susceptible cultivars, you will need to begin a preventive spray program in mid-spring. Wettable

Blackspot is one of the most serious diseases of roses. Choose resistant cultivars whenever possible.

sulfur powder provides reasonably good protection and does not have the toxicity of fungicides like Captan or Benlate, although it does not have the residual property of these fungicides. Spray after each rain or wet period, and use a few drops of a liquid soap in your sprayer to help spread the sulfur evenly over the foliage. Without a spreader the sulfur will tend to bead and roll off the leaves. We also use a solution of 40 parts water to one part hydrogen peroxide as a preventative spray. With this you will need to add a few drops of a pure soap to act as a sticker. Another old remedy uses baking soda (sodium bicarbonate) as a preventive spray. Mix 1 oz. (30 g) of baking soda in 10 gal. (40 L) of water and apply after damp periods. I assume the baking soda changes the acidity of the leaf surface, making it an inhospitable place for fungi to grow.

Some wonderful breeding work has been done in the past 70 years to develop blackspot resistance. Some of the most important early work was carried out by Wilhelm Kordes of Germany. Using a particularly resistant seedling, Kordes bred numerous roses, including some reasonably hardy modern shrub types that are quite resistant to blackspot. Felicitas Svejda of Agriculture Canada also concentrated much of her efforts on disease resistance, and the results, called the Explorer Series, are nearly all resistant to blackspot. More programs such as the Canadian Artist Series and the 49th Parallel Series have made great strides in disease resistance. Several programs in Europe and the United States are also using resistance as a critical criterion for introduction.

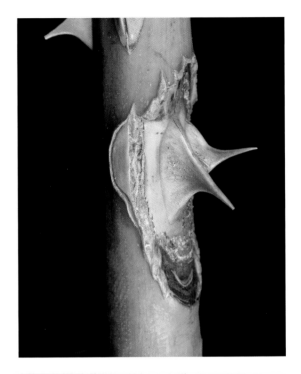

Canker should be removed as soon as it is noticed.

Canker (*Coniothyrium* spp.)

Cankers usually appear as the result of poor sanitation and pruning. The cankers show up as brown or orange spots on dead wood and then spread to the adjacent live wood. By pruning out dead wood, canker can be almost wholly prevented. Use sharp bypass pruning shears that will not tear wood, and cut cleanly and closely to the nearest live branch. Burn canker when it is found or put it in an actively working compost pile. Dip your pruning shears in isopropyl alcohol frequently to avoid spreading the disease.

Frog Eye (*Cercospora rosicola*)

The common name for this disease is quite descriptive. This fungal disease shows up on a

Crown gall can reduce vigor in a plant. Inspect your new roses before planting to ensure they are not infected.

leaf as a circle of purple or maroon, and it soon develops a necrotic central spot that is tan to nearly translucent. In mild, damp weather and where water stays on the leaves, the disease can spread rapidly. It is wise to remove any affected leaves as soon as frog eye is noticed and, when possible, avoid overhead watering of the plants. A spray of wettable sulfur just after the leaves unfold can help prevent infection; just be careful not to use sulfur on hot sunny days, as it may burn the leaves' tissues.

Crown Gall
(Agrobacterium tumefaciens)

Crown gall is found on the roots of roses and related plants. It is caused by a species of bacteria that is found in nearly all soils and that gains entrance through a mechanical injury or insect damage. The galls are irregular, bulbous growths, which over time can become quite large. There is some debate over how much crown gall harms the plants it infects, but the consensus is that it does affect the vigor and longevity of the plant. Do not use gall-infected plants if you can avoid it. If for some reason you have to use a plant that shows galls, cut off the infected roots. A biological control for crown gall is now available. Before planting, the roots are dipped into a solution of water and *Agrobacterium radiobacter*, another species of bacteria that inhibits the growth of the crown gall bacteria. This specific bacteria is quite safe to use and extremely effective. Be sure to follow the instructions and do not allow the bacteria to be exposed to sunlight for any amount of time.

Powdery Mildew
(*Podosphaera pannosa*)

Powdery mildew shows up as a grayish-white coating on the surface of infected leaves. It is particularly troublesome in late summer. Susceptible roses can be severely harmed unless measures are taken.

Mildew, as is the case with so many diseases, tends to show up on stressed plants more than on healthy ones. Roses that are either poorly nourished or overstimulated by heavy feeding of nitrogen fertilizers are particularly prone to mildew. Plants that do not receive enough water are likewise affected. Keep your plant mulched and well fed with compost. This will promote a balanced growth that will help to prevent mildew. Place susceptible cultivars in areas where they will get good air circulation. If you are growing a particularly susceptible rose, you may find it necessary to adopt a spray program using wettable sulfur. A solution of hydrogen peroxide and sodium bicarbonate can be used as well.

Rust (*Phragmidium tuberculatum*)

Rust is a fungal disease that attacks young stems in early summer. Orange pustules form and spread spores, which appear as orange spots, across the underside of the leaves. These can spread more spores to other roses. In the fall black spores are produced that can rest for the winter on leaves, stems or even trellises and other nearby objects.

This disease does not seem to be as prevalent in northern areas. This may reflect a difference in the type of roses grown, or perhaps rust is unable to overwinter in colder temperatures.

Research your choice of rose to see if it is subject to mildew. Healthy, well-watered plants will be more resistant.

Most modern shrub roses are resistant to rust. We occasionally see it on some of the *Rosa alba* cultivars.

If you notice rust, immediately remove and burn or bury any infected foliage. Infected leaves should likewise be removed from the ground to prevent reinfection. A new layer of mulch will help prevent dropped leaves from dispersing spores into the air. With a bit of diligence this disease can be prevented from becoming a problem.

Viruses

Viruses are organisms that show up throughout the animal and plant world. Virus-infected roses will show symptoms such as yellowed and streaked leaves. The flowers of a virus-infected rose may be small and few, and foliage may drop prematurely. A reliable test when you are wondering if a rose has a virus is to inspect the streaking on the leaves. If the streaking is

Rust can infect certain cultivars, particularly in warmer climates. Remove any affected portions immediately so the spores cannot spread the disease.

symmetrical (same on both side of the central vein), you have a virus-infected plant. You cannot cure a virus. It is most often spread when infected stock is used for nursery propagation. If you are sure you have a virus-infected rose, and not simply a rose that is suffering from pests, lack of water or nutritional deficiencies, rip it out. Sucking insects such as aphids can spread the virus to healthy plants.

Reading through a section on insects and diseases can be disheartening. Please, do not be discouraged. Our gardens are never sprayed, with the possible exception of a little sulfur on a few blackspot-susceptible cultivars, and we have no serious problems. Keep your garden well tended, spend time building healthy soil and choose healthy cultivars when possible, and you will be rewarded with healthy roses.

5 PROPAGATION

Rose petals littered across the floor and the gentle click of pruning shears are some of the sights and sounds that surround me when working at my favorite pastime — propagation. The creation of new plants is one of the great pleasures of the horticultural world and is for me the primary reason for being a nurseryman. Propagation lies at the very foundation of horticulture. Whether from seed, cuttings, grafting or budding, the result is the same — a new generation of plants. Through centuries of trial and error, propagators have discovered the easiest ways to produce the many plants that gardeners have been interested in growing. A great deal of effort has been devoted to the rose.

◀ There are few things as satisfying as producing new plants from seed, from cuttings or by budding.

Several methods of propagation are used. Each method has its merits and problems. Some methods work for some roses and not for others. The problem of growing roses in the north throws a curve into the equation, and it is my contention that getting hardy roses on their own roots is a decided advantage. Be that as it may, all the methods described in this chapter can be successfully used to produce roses.

If you are curious about how roses are produced, or if you are interested in producing your own plants, the following section describes the various techniques in some detail. If you are not interested in the actual propagation procedures, please feel free to skip this section.

GROWING FROM SEED

Growing roses from seed is the oldest form of propagation. As the petals of a rose unfold, the female part of the flower, the pistil, becomes receptive to fertilization by pollen, which is found at the top of the male structures, called stamens, that surround the pistil. Fertilization can occur between the flowers of the same plant (this would produce a "selfed" seedling), but more often fertilization occurs between two different plants; therefore, the seed contains characteristics of both parents. These differences are usually minor within a species, although occasionally a seedling will differ substantially from the general type.

Breeders often use species roses (roses belonging to a distinct species) to inject hardiness into their breeding line. More often than not the species rose will be used as the female parent, as species roses tend to have better seed production than rose cultivars.

If you would like to try growing roses from seeds, collect them in the fall when the hips are fully ripe. You can test for ripeness

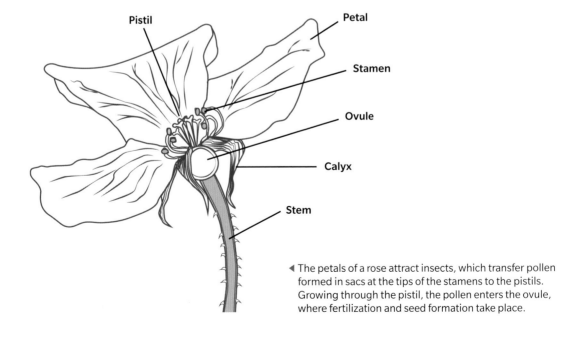

Pistil

Petal

Stamen

Ovule

Calyx

Stem

◀ The petals of a rose attract insects, which transfer pollen formed in sacs at the tips of the stamens to the pistils. Growing through the pistil, the pollen enters the ovule, where fertilization and seed formation take place.

The seeds within a rose hip are surrounded by an edible layer that attracts animals, which can then spread the seeds far and wide.

by opening the hip. The seeds inside should have turned a deep tan to dark brown. Immature seeds will appear whitish or very light tan. Once collected, rose seeds, particularly from hardy species or cultivars, will require a period of cool, moist conditions called stratification. Seeds can be planted directly into prepared earth beds or trays in the fall. If you use trays, put these in a place where they will remain near the freezing point until spring. Be sure the seeds are protected from mice, which will make short work of your seeds.

Another method is to mix one part seed to at least three parts of a barely damp, sterile medium such as peat moss. Place the mix into a sealed polyethylene bag. Put this in a refrigerator and keep just above freezing for three or four months. Be careful not to keep fruit, such as apples, in the same refrigerator, as stored fruit gives off ethylene gas, which may injure the seed.

Germination should be prompt once the seeds are planted in a container and placed in warmer temperatures, although you should be aware that successful germination rates for rose seeds are often disappointingly low.

Seeds collected from rose cultivars will produce seedlings that are different from the parent. It is exciting to see what results you may get from what is called "open pollination." Many roses have been created in this manner. In the horticultural world seeds are used mainly for the propagation of species roses, but all breeding depends upon seeds. The bulk of breeding work today involves the crossing of selected parents.

Rose breeders have a curious but fascinating job. By crossing two cultivars/species with desirable characteristics, they try to create roses with the combination of traits they want. This process may involve a series of crosses, referred to as F1, F2 and F3 generations. A breeding program may involve many generations of crosses, meaning years or decades of work. With each new cross it is hoped the breeder creates seedlings that are closer to their goal.

The technique of breeding is simple, but proper timing and delicate hand work are needed to ensure good results. To cross two roses, first choose the female or seed parent. This parent must be a fertile cultivar. Fertile roses form fruit (rose hips). Carefully remove all the petals from the flowers of your seed parent the day before they open. With tweezers, carefully remove the tops of the stamens, which contain the pollen. Gently place a small paper bag over each emasculated flower for approximately 24 hours to prevent unwanted pollen from fertilizing them, then examine the pistils. When they are slightly sticky, they are receptive.

In order to have pollen for your cross, you will need to choose and cut flowers from your male that are newly open. Most breeders place the flower upside down on a piece of glassine paper in a dry warm room. By day's end there should be a small quantity of pollen on the sheet, which can be kept in a small vial or in the folded glassine. Obviously, the more pollen you can collect, the better.

Remove the paper bag from the female parent, and gently brush the pollen on the pistils of the female parent. This is usually done on a warm afternoon. A fine sable brush is the best tool for this job. If you are using several different male parents, be sure to carefully wash out the brush with alcohol and dry thoroughly before you change pollen sources. Cover the flower with the paper bag again. After a week or two the fruit will begin to swell if fertilization has been successful. Remove the bags and carefully mark each flower, noting the male parent used for the cross.

Harvest the seeds when the fruit changes color from green to red or orange, depending on the cultivar. Waiting to harvest as long as possible in the fall will ensure the seeds are ripe, but do not allow them to stay in temperatures below freezing point. Open the fruits and take out the seeds. Ripe seeds will be deep tan or brown. Unripe seeds will be white, and usually these will not be viable.

Although few people have the patience for breeding roses, and even fewer have the time and money required for a major breeding program, innumerable roses have been created by enthusiastic amateurs. Most seedlings you produce will probably be roses of little horticultural value, but the dream of creating that special new rose keeps the breeder ever hopeful. And even if you do not create the rose of the century, the process and results can be satisfying in themselves.

LAYERING

As a rosebush grows, it often sends out underground stems called stolons, or more colloquially, "suckers." By digging these out and cutting them off from the main plant, you can easily create new plants. Among the northern roses, *Rosa rugosa* is well known for its suckering nature, and these suckers are a simple way to produce a few plants from the original. You will be most successful if the suckers are taken in early spring and the above-ground portion of the sucker is pruned to a short stub.

Be careful when taking suckers from a budded or grafted plant. The rootstock will be totally different from the cultivar on top. A careful examination of the leaves will usually show any differences. Even if a rose does not readily produce suckers, however, the process of layering offers an opportunity to the propagator.

Layering involves bending down a stem and burying it several inches into the soil with the tip protruding. A metal or wooden stake may be required to keep the layer from popping out of the ground. Be sure to keep the layer well covered and damp. Some propagators wound the portion to be buried by making a knife

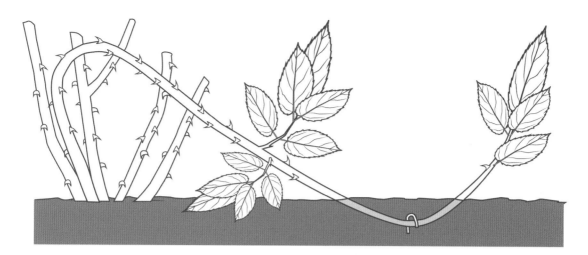

Burying a stem underground simulates roots to form. Later, the layer tip, with its new roots, can be severed from the mother plant and planted.

cut perpendicular to the stem before burying the layer to promote root production. Hard-to-root cultivars may also benefit from the application of a rooting hormone such as IBA (indole-3-butyric acid) to the wound.

The buried portion will eventually form roots. If layered in the spring, most layers will have formed enough roots so you can remove them by early the next spring. A few cultivars may require longer periods. When digging up these layers be careful not to injure the delicate new roots. To remove from the parent plant, cut the base of the layer cleanly off with snips, and if the top is long, cut it back to only a few buds. Plant and water well. In the north, early spring is best for this.

This technique is easy and reliable, particularly for the home gardener, as it takes no special equipment or structures. The commercial grower faces the problem of producing large numbers of plants. To accomplish this, many growers bud their roses.

BUDDING

Budding is the preferred technique of most commercial growers. Although it requires some practice to master the art of budding, it is essentially a simple process and can easily be performed by anyone with enough interest and a sharp knife.

Budding is the placing of a bud from the desired cultivar onto a rootstock. Several rootstocks are in general use today, though most growers in Europe and North America use either *Rosa multiflora* or *Rosa canina*. "Thornless" cultivars (cultivars without prickles) of these species are preferred.

The rootstocks are grown for one or two years either in the field or in containers. Budding is usually performed during the period of active growth, which in most northern areas is between late July and mid-August. Prepare the rootstocks by cleaning off any soil adhering to the stems. With a sharp, thin-bladed knife, make a T-shaped incision 1 to 2 in. (2.5 to 5 cm) from the soil line; the cuts should slice through the bark, no deeper. Pry back the two corner flaps to insert the bud.

Single vegetative buds of the desired cultivar are cut from a prepared stem, which has had its leaves removed with only a short section

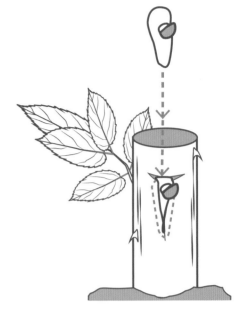
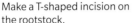

Make a T-shaped incision on the rootstock.

Remove a bud of the desired cultivar.

After removing the inner wood of the cut bud, insert it into the T-shaped incision and bind it in place.

of the leaf petioles attached to the stem. (The petiole will act as a handle when inserting the bud.) Cut just slightly into the woody portion of the stem; the resulting shape is somewhat shield-like. Carefully remove the woody portion under the bud, so that only the bark and the bud itself remain. Insert the bud, pointing naturally upward, into the incision.

After positioning, bind the bud to the rootstock by wrapping it with an elastic band or a latex tie especially made for the purpose. This wrapping ensures that there is good contact between the bud and rootstock, and prevents air from getting into the wound and drying out the bud before it has a chance to unite with the stock. After a month, remove these ties and examine the bud. If it has taken it will be green and swollen. If not, it will be blackened and dead. In very early spring cut the rootstock stem just above the new bud. This cut should slope slightly down and away from the bud. As

the bud grows, rub off any suckers from the rootstock. If not removed, these will use much of the plant's strength.

Budding has several advantages. The use of an established rootstock furnishes the bud with tremendous vigor, and a sizable plant can be produced in a single year. The use of rootstocks also imparts vigor into cultivars that, on their own roots, would remain smaller. Perhaps the major advantage, from a grower's point of view, is that a plant can be produced from a single bud. This means that the required number of stock plants from which the buds are taken is relatively small.

There are disadvantages as well. A budded plant remains two separate plants. The rootstock is quite different from the top cultivar. Often the rootstock will send up suckers, and the flowers on these suckers will be completely different. A double red rose suddenly has small single white flowers in its midst. Gardeners not familiar with how roses are produced often say, "My rose has gone wild." Though the flowers may be pretty, most gardeners do not want the rootstock suckers, and removing them is a constant problem that must be attended to with budded roses. A second disadvantage is a more serious problem, particularly for growers living in hardiness Zone 4 and colder. The most common rose rootstocks are not reliably hardy in the far north. Even though the top cultivar may be perfectly hardy, you can lose your plant if the rootstock suffers winterkill. Without an insulating layer of snow, frost penetrates deeply into the ground, and temperatures may fall below what the rootstock can tolerate. This is especially troublesome in areas that do not receive reliable snow cover.

Roses produced by budding are the most common type of rose sold. If you are planting such a rose be sure to place the bud union (the swollen area just above the roots) 2 to 4 in. (5 to 10 cm) beneath the soil surface. This will prevent light, which initiates suckering, from reaching the rootstock. As well, it will give the cultivar a chance to form roots of its own, thereby making the plant less dependent upon the survival of the rootstock. In heavier clay soils, planting deeply may at first reduce the rose's vigor because oxygen levels will be lower, but as roots form on the upper sections, vigor will return. Plants that are pruned heavily will tend to sucker more. The reduction of the top stimulates dormant buds on the rootstock into growth, to try to replace the lost leaf area. To prevent unwanted suckering from the rootstock it is, therefore, advantageous to keep any pruning of the desired cultivar to a minimum.

GRAFTING

Grafting and budding accomplish the same task. Only the technique differs. Instead of placing a bud under the bark, a section of stem is placed on top of the rootstock.

Grafting is usually done on dormant rootstocks in winter or very early spring. Several different methods are used to join the cultivar to the rootstock. The most commonly used are the whip-and-tongue graft and the wedge graft.

Two things are absolutely necessary to the success of grafting. You must have a razor-sharp, thin-bladed knife and tough fingers. Rose prickles are difficult to deal with at the best of times, but they can be a real nuisance when you're grafting. I find it extremely difficult to graft while wearing gloves. Grafting requires dexterity, and gloves just get in the way. However, if you have thin leather gloves, you may find them useful. Many roses have prickles that are easily removed by gently pressing them sideways. Your job will be much easier with such roses.

To make a whip-and-tongue graft, cut the rootstock with a sharp blade just above the roots at an angle that leaves the length of the exposed surface about two times the diameter of the stock. Halfway down the cut, and with the blade pointing down the slope, make a second cut. When making this cut raise the blade just slightly from the surface, so that a thin flap is created. This cut should be no longer than one-quarter the length of the exposed surface of the initial cut. Using a section of stem containing one to three buds, make the same sequence of cuts on the

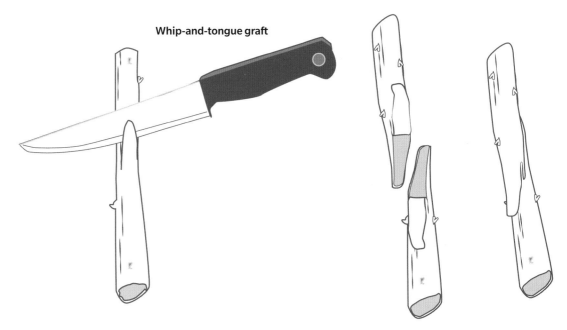

Whip-and-tongue graft

Healthy material, a sharp knife to make flat, clean cuts, and good alignment of the cambium (inner bark) are the essential elements of successful grafting.

bottom of the piece from the desired cultivar. This piece is referred to as the scion. Slide the scion down onto the rootstock. The thin flaps at the center of each cut should lock the two pieces. Fit them gently and snugly together. If the cuts are flat and the flaps are thin, there should be good surface-to-surface contact. When you fit the graft, it is essential that at least one side of the union have the cambiums aligned. (The cambium is the thin green layer just under the bark.) This is where cell division occurs and, therefore, where the two sections will knit together. Without proper alignment, the cells will not be able to connect, and the graft will fail. If the scion and rootstock are different sizes, make certain at least one side is aligned.

Once you have locked the two pieces together, bind them snugly with a budding rubber, masking tape or parafilm, a stretchy,

self-adhesive waxy plastic material that is ideal for grafting. When tying, be careful not to shift the alignment. Once tied, brush on or dip into a pot of warm grafting wax to seal the graft. This will prevent the graft from drying out before healing takes place. Several grafting waxes are available on the market. If you are unable to find a commercial preparation, melted paraffin wax will work. We make up our own mix of one part rosin to three parts beeswax. This must be heated to be workable. (Rosin, which is the hardened gum of certain pines, is becoming increasingly difficult to find.) Place your grafts in a cool place until you are ready to plant. Be sure that the roots are kept slightly moist.

There is a variation of the wedge grafting process that we have found very useful. This technique is used in the greenhouse, but it could be adapted to a cold frame or humidity tent. We collect sticks of both the desired rootstock and the cultivar in late spring and early summer. Only slightly hardened, new

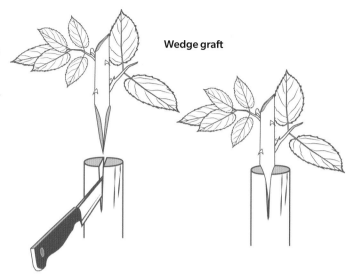

Wedge graft

This is a simple and effective method of grafting, particularly on small material in the greenhouse. ▶

wood is used, and this should be vigorous and reasonably thick. First remove the leaves from the rootstock sticks. Cut these sticks into sections 3 to 4 in. (8 to 10 cm) long, being sure to keep track of which ends are top and which bottom. Using a sharp knife, make a vertical cut down into the center of the top of a rootstock section. This cut should only be 0.5 in. (1.3 cm) deep. Next cut a section of the cultivar stick, leaving two or three leaves on each section. Slice the base of the cultivar section into a 0.75 in. (2 cm) long wedge. Using the tip of the knife to open the top of the rootstock section slightly, insert the wedged end of the cultivar into the cut, aligning the cambium layers as you do so. Push the wedge far enough so that it is snug, but not so far that it will split the rootstock section. If properly made, the graft will be snug enough without needing to be tied.

Dip the basal end of the completed graft into a rooting hormone. We usually use a 0.2 percent IBA (indole-3-butyric acid) talc powder preparation, but a similar strength liquid hormone will work. Be sure to place the hormone only on the very tip. Too much hormone on the stem will burn the cutting. Gently stick the cutting into a rooting medium, which should be clean and perfectly drained. A mixture of four parts perlite to one part peat works well. Clean sand will work as well. If kept sufficiently moist and warm, the grafted cutting will root within two or three weeks. Once rooted it can be potted up until it is sufficiently acclimatized to be planted outdoors.

Grafting is a reasonably simple and rewarding technique for producing roses. Like budding, it creates plants that are the union of two different cultivars, and the problems of suckering and rootstock hardiness are the same. On the whole, grafting is somewhat more reliable than budding when done on rootstocks growing in the field, since newly budded roses can suffer winterkill in areas with very low winter temperatures, especially when there is no snow cover. Grafting is one of the oldest propagating methods for roses, and it is still one of the most dependable.

GROWING FROM CUTTINGS

Nearly all cultivars of roses can be rooted from cuttings. Some are easy to root, while others are difficult. Most fall in the middle. Yet this simple technique is rarely used by commercial growers because budding and grafting methods are more economically advantageous.

There are two general types of cuttings — softwood and hardwood. The names refer to the condition of the wood when the cuttings are taken. Softwood cuttings are taken in early summer, when the wood is actively growing and fairly soft. Hardwood cuttings are taken when the plants are dormant, and the wood is quite firm. The vast majority of rose cuttings are softwood. It is my experience that hardwood cutting propagation in the north is usually unsuccessful. In England, where winter temperatures are mild, hardwood cuttings are stuck directly in the ground in fall and usually root by spring. In our cold winters, this technique usually fails, and we confine our work to softwood cuttings.

The process of rooting rose cuttings is quite simple. What is needed is an understanding of the environmental requirements necessary to keep the cutting healthy until it is ready to be put out as a rooted plant.

Collect softwood cuttings as soon as the first flower buds form in early summer. Cuttings taken from stems that are just about to flower consistently have the highest percentage of rooting. Gather your cuttings when conditions are cool. Early morning is the best time, as the stems have not been wilted by the sun. Never let cuttings dry out. Move them quickly into a cool place and sprinkle them with water immediately.

Take great care in selecting your cuttings. You will not succeed without healthy cuttings. Cuttings should be collected from well-fed, actively growing and disease-free plants. A healthy cutting has an adequate supply of nutrients in its tissues to sustain it until it roots. Diseases or insects can interfere with the cutting's ability to function properly. Cuttings with insects such as aphids on them can cause

Use only enough rooting hormone to cover the base of the cutting. Using more will burn the tissues.

havoc in the greenhouse. We soak all cuttings for a few minutes in an insecticidal soap dip before rinsing them. Insecticidal soaps are nontoxic to mammals, but kill soft-bodied insects in short order.

The availability of material and the number of plants you want to produce determine how large a cutting you take. Most roses will form roots on small cuttings with only one or two leaves. If material is available though, larger cuttings are preferable. A cutting 4 to 8 in. (10 to 20 cm) long will initially make a much stronger plant than a smaller cutting. Be sure to cut any flowers or flower buds off the tips. Dip the freshly cut base of the cutting in rooting hormone. When using talc preparations of rooting hormone, be sure to dip only the very bottom of the cuttings in the hormone and shake off any excess. Too much hormone can burn them. When using liquid hormone preparations, be sure to dip the base only for as long as recommended. Softwood

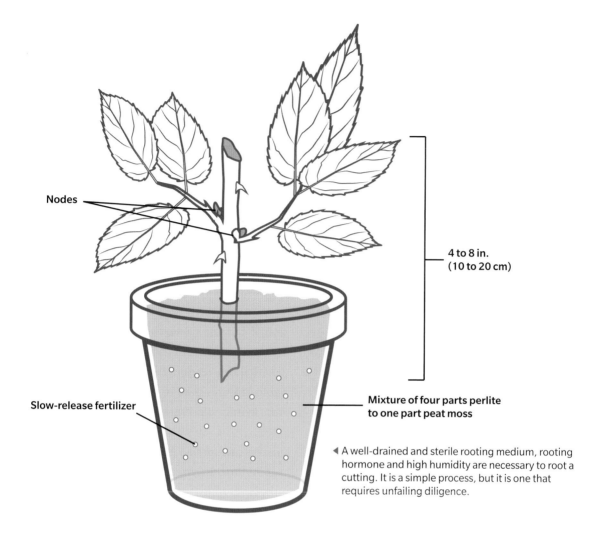

Nodes

4 to 8 in.
(10 to 20 cm)

Slow-release fertilizer

Mixture of four parts perlite
to one part peat moss

◄ A well-drained and sterile rooting medium, rooting
hormone and high humidity are necessary to root a
cutting. It is a simple process, but it is one that
requires unfailing diligence.

rose cuttings do not require a strong hormone concentration. Use a 0.2 percent IBA (indole-3-butyric acid) preparation (commonly sold as "#2"). Stronger concentrations can burn the cutting.

Stick the cuttings in a rooting medium. A rooting medium serves two purposes. It holds the cutting in place and provides enough moisture around the base to aid the rooting process. Excessive moisture, however, can cause the base to rot. The ideal medium, therefore, has perfect drainage yet holds enough water to keep the cutting moist.

One option that works as a rooting medium is a mixture of four parts perlite to one part peat moss. Most references I have read recommend one part perlite or sand to one part peat, but our experiences with rooting mediums like these were disastrous. We lost crop after crop from rot. We gradually decreased the peat content until we arrived at the four to one ratio. The roses will root in straight perlite, but once roots form they seem to need some organic material to toughen up. Peat provides a relatively sterile source of organics. Cuttings grown in straight perlite do not seem to survive transplanting as well as cuttings grown in a perlite-peat mixture. Although perlite is an ideal material, if you cannot obtain it, you can use clean sand. Sand has been the material of choice for centuries. Just be sure it has no organic residues. These organics can harbor pathogens, which can cause rotting.

Today at the nursery we stick our cuttings in clean sand mixed with 10 percent screened peat moss. We spread a layer of the sand mix 4 in. (10 cm) thick on the concrete floor of the greenhouse. The advantage of having a layer like this is that the roots are not constrained by the walls of a container, which creates a perfect spreading root system.

A great deal has been written about the use of fertilizers in rooting mediums. The rooting medium itself is relatively sterile; therefore, when the cutting roots there are no nutrients to absorb, and the cutting essentially feeds off itself. Organic fertilizers such as compost present problems when used in rooting mediums, for they can contain life forms that may feed on the injured portions of the cutting and may eventually cause rot. It would seem that fertilizer added to the medium might help to feed the cutting until it can be potted up in a soil mix. However, free nitrogen in the medium before the cutting has rooted promotes the growth of a range of microscopic life forms, some of which will feed on the injured tissues at the base of the cutting and increase the likelihood of rot.

The compromise we have adopted is to use a slow-release form of fertilizer that is activated by moisture and temperature. These fertilizers are made of granules coated by a thin layer that releases the nutrients gradually throughout the growing season. Although not as readily available as the more common fertilizers, slow-release fertilizers can be found in many garden centers and nurseries.

When mixed in very small quantities in the rooting medium, a slow-release fertilizer can be very beneficial. When the cuttings are first stuck, the coating around the individual grains of fertilizer prevents any appreciable amount of nutrient from escaping into the medium. When the first roots appear after about two weeks, the levels of fertilizer are sufficient to provide nutrients to the new roots. Before we began using this slow-release formula, many of our cuttings would form roots, then drop their leaves and die. The use of a slow-release fertilizer prevents this, and the cuttings are able to begin growth as soon as roots emerge.

Creating the proper environment for cuttings is critical to the success of the whole operation. What the propagator needs to achieve is a humidity level that is high enough to prevent the cutting from wilting, yet not so wet that it will saturate the rooting medium and leach out nutrients from the leaves. Several innovations in propagation equipment have provided commercial growers with systems that create a foggy or fog-like environment in the greenhouse. These systems spray a very fine mist that floats in the air and surrounds the cuttings with moisture without soaking the cuttings and medium. The older type of overhead mist nozzles use more water and tend to keep the cuttings so wet that they run with water. This system can be used with success, but it is not as desirable.

Most gardeners do not have fancy systems or greenhouses in which to propagate their cuttings; however, there is a simple alternative. A small cold frame structure that is essentially a box with an angled transparent top can be a great structure for rooting cuttings. Old storm windows are ideal for the top. By placing it on the north side of your house, it will not receive direct sun, which can heat up the interior and raise temperatures to dangerous levels, thereby drying out the cuttings. During the daylight hours, keep the cuttings slightly damp. A fine misting nozzle works well. If the cold frame is tight, the humidity can be kept high with only a few light mistings each day. Hot days may require more. Once the cuttings begin to root, the top of the cold frame can be raised slightly for short periods until the cuttings become acclimatized to the drier atmosphere, at which point they can be transplanted or left over winter and transplanted in spring.

Temperature is important in determining how speedily your cuttings will root. Reasonably high temperatures will speed the process of cell activity. Once above 88°F (30°C), however, growth slows down. Higher temperatures can be detrimental to the cuttings. Cuttings that have been allowed to dry even for as short a time as 15 minutes may be irreparably damaged. This is why many amateur propagators fail in their attempts to root roses. The process is simple, but constant vigilance is essential for success.

Heat from below can also be an advantage when rooting cuttings. This heat can be provided by hot water pipes or electric resistance cable run in the bed under the cuttings. A constant temperature of 70 to 77°F (22 to 25°C) is ideal. We have found that *Rosa rugosa* hybrids respond well to bottom heat, particularly when cuttings are taken early in the growing season.

Once the cuttings have produced several strong roots, they can be potted. Move your newly transplanted roses into an area where you can water frequently to help the new plants gradually adjust to the drier atmosphere. Many plants are lost at this stage, and nothing hurts more than to have gone through all the trials of rooting your cuttings only to see them dry up after transplanting. It is also a good idea to partially shade your newly rooted plants to keep temperatures from becoming too high and drying out the leaves. At this point the leaves are "lazy." On their undersides are small pores, called stomata, that open and close to regulate the amount of water in the leaves. In the high humidity of a greenhouse or cold frame they seem to grow sluggish and do not respond as rapidly to changes in humidity levels. If the plant is put in the hot sun and the stomata stay open, the moisture in the leaves escapes and they dry up. If given several days of slow adjustment after removal from the greenhouse or cold frame, however, the leaves start functioning normally and are ready to face the harsh realities of sun, wind and heat.

If you wish you can plant your rooted cuttings into their final place in the garden, but do so only after you have given them the adjustment period mentioned above. Keep them well watered and be sure to mulch them before cold weather. This will keep the roots insulated. Once established in the soil, the rose will need only routine care.

It may be safer to leave the cuttings in your greenhouse or cold frame over winter. They will be better rooted by spring and will not have undergone the shock of transplanting just before winter. If you are leaving them to overwinter in a small, low cold frame, it is advisable to cover the cold frame with some sort of insulation. Ideally, use insulation board fitted to the inside of the frame. Be sure to leave some mouse bait, as mice may find a way in to dine on your newly rooted cuttings.

You may need to pot your overwintered cuttings in early spring once they initiate growth, particularly if they have been kept in a relatively warm greenhouse and are beginning growth earlier than they would outside. If your roses are in full leaf by spring, be sure to wait until the danger of frost is over. If they are just beginning to bud you can plant as soon as outdoor conditions are right for planting. Do not wait too long, though. Roses bud very early and can be quite frost resistant. Essentially, this means that if their growth is in sync with the outdoor roses, you can plant your rooted cuttings as soon as the frost leaves the ground and the soil becomes workable.

It is my contention that a rose on its own roots is a superior plant, particularly when placed in a northern garden setting. The aggravating problem of rootstock suckering disappears. The problem of incompatibility between the rootstock and the cultivar is nonexistent.

Most importantly, you need only worry about the hardiness of the cultivar. Many roses that can be grown in the far north are far more hardy than the rootstocks on which they are budded. You are less likely to lose your rose to winter injury as a result of rootstock injury. As well, the rootstock can influence the hardening-off process in the fall. The more tender rootstocks will keep the cultivar growing longer into the fall than the cultivar might if it were on its own roots.

Another factor that is perhaps overlooked by most rose growers is the rootstock's influence on vigor. In many cases increased vigor is not an advantage, particularly when you are seeking a rose for a small space. Many dwarf or low-growing roses become far larger plants when pushed by their rootstocks. By propagating roses on their own roots, you can be more certain of their ultimate size. These factors make the time and trouble involved in rooting roses worthwhile.

It is a regrettable fact that roses on their own roots are very difficult to find in the nursery trade, although more are being produced. For the northern grower it is worth the search. But if you have the inclination and the time, and you can put together the facilities, the challenging and rewarding process of rooting roses can let you produce your own. There is no finer feeling than the pleasure of watching the first blossom unfurling on a rosebush that you have helped create.

Rosa multiflora is one of the most commonly used ▶ rootstocks for roses.

PART 2

THE CULTIVARS: PETALS OF LIGHT

◀ Oscar Peterson is one of the fine new cultivars that show outstanding resistance to disease.

INTRODUCTORY NOTES

For each cultivar I am profiling, I have included a box with the following information:

Hardiness Zones: The hardiness zone given for each rose indicates the northern limit for growing that cultivar. This does not mean you cannot grow the rose in a colder area, but you can expect severe winter injury without some form of insulation.

There are two hardiness zone maps for Canada and one for the United States: Canada's Plant Hardiness Zones, Canada's Extreme Minimum Temperature Zones and the USDA Plant Hardiness Zone Map. The second Canadian map, Canada's Extreme Minimum Temperature Zones, follows the same approach as the USDA map, and for that reason we've included these two maps in the appendix. There is little difference between Canada's Plant Hardiness Zones and Canada's Extreme Minimum Temperature Zones, with slight exceptions when looking at Zones 3, 4 and 5. I originally assigned the hardiness zones using Canada's Plant Hardiness Zones; however, in most instances the hardiness zone will be close to or the same as Canada's Extreme Minimum Temperature Zones and the USDA Plant Hardiness Zone Map.

Introduced: This is the date a rose was introduced to horticulture. The rose may have been grown several years earlier, but the date indicates when the first reference to the cultivar appeared. Dates can vary depending on the source.

Origin: This is the surname of the breeder or discoverer and the country where the selection or discovery took place.

Parentage: The parents of most cultivars are usually provided by the breeder. The parentage of some roses is unknown, as they may have been discovered as seedlings or the breeder did not disclose the parents. In these cases the parents are listed as unknown and/or a parentage surmised by rose experts.

I've used the abbreviation "o.p." to denote when a cultivar was open pollinated, meaning the seed from which the cultivar has grown is a result of a parent plant that was pollinated naturally. Consequently, the female parent is known but the pollen parent is unknown.

Height: The ultimate heights given reflect our experience with the rose. Height can vary, sometimes markedly, with site, climate, soil and nurturing methods. Please note I have given only approximations when giving equivalent heights in imperial and metric. For example, if a rose grows 3 ft. tall I would give an equivalent of 1 m. Mathematicians will cringe, I am sure, as 3 ft. is actually 0.9144 m, but these are only general guides, anyway.

Fragrance: The perfume of a rose is a difficult thing to rate. Not only is scent influenced by time of day and temperature, but also every person's nose is different. Some may consider a rose fragrant while others would say not. I have used my nose as a guide and assigned the following ratings:
  f — little or no fragrance
  ff — lightly fragrant
  fff — fragrant
  ffff — exceptionally fragrant

◀ Champlain, an early Explorer Series rose, is a prolific bloomer.

6 CLIMBERS

Shrubs growing taller than 7 ft. (2 m) and suitable for tying on supports

◀ This very double Quadra has been trained alongside an apple we have espaliered against the wall.

AÏCHA

Hardiness Zone: 3b
Introduced: 1966
Origin: Petersen, Denmark
Parentage: Souvenir de Jacques
  Verschuren × Guldtop
Height: 8 ft. (2.5 m)
Fragrance: fff

that is perfectly happy to spend the winter in the chill wind. In all the years we have grown this rose it has never failed to perform, and I can recommend it without hesitation for northern growers.

The gently arching stems create a nicely shaped bush if you prefer not to use it as a climber, and those with a nose for fragrance will delight in the perfume of this dazzling rose. We were surprised that after several years in the garden we started to see some repeat blooms. While these cannot compete with the first flush, it is delightful to discover a few new treasures exploding like daytime fireworks in midsummer.

This is an easy rose to grow, with healthy deep green foliage, but it is moderately difficult to propagate from cuttings. It is important that the cuttings be taken at the beginning of the flowering season. Be careful not to keep the cuttings overly wet or they will drop their leaves. This rose is more commonly budded or layered.

You may have difficulty finding this rose, but you should make the effort. Even on a cloudy day the cheerful petals of Aïcha bring a welcome burst of sunshine into the garden, and you will be amply rewarded for the time spent obtaining it.

When the first blooms on my plants opened, I was intrigued by their distinctive form and dazzled by their sunshine-yellow color. I would visit the plants daily to watch the newest buds unfurl and the older flowers pale to the color of buttermilk.

Each flower's immense outer petals cradle five inner petals, which in turn encircle the largest grouping of stamens I have seen in a rose. Even after the petals drop, the reddish stamens remain attractive and fascinating. The flowers are borne on vigorous and prickly stems that can be trained to form a spectacular climber, one

AMES CLIMBER

Hardiness Zone: 3a
Introduced: 1932
Origin: Maney, USA
Parentage: *Rosa multiflora* Thun.
　× *Rosa blanda* Aiton
Height: 10 ft. (3 m)
Fragrance: f

Although an older cultivar, this rose has never been produced and distributed in any meaningful quantity. This is partially due to the fact that it is a one-time bloomer. We were sent cuttings by Margit Schowalter, a collector of rare Canadian heritage roses, and were impressed by Ames Climber's vigor, toughness and excellent show.

When in bloom it attracts attention with its bounteous blooms. The single flowers are relatively large with a sizable boss of yellow stamens. Pink buds open white blushed pink, then age to pure white. The foliage is heavily textured, a sign of its *multiflora* heritage. It is extremely disease resistant.

Though poorly known, this is a good rose to seek out, particularly if you live on a very cold site. It lends itself well to growing on a trellis and makes a very attractive climber.

This rose roots well.

CAPTAIN SAMUEL HOLLAND

Captain Samuel Holland charted the coasts of Maritime Canada in the 16th century. It is likely that this new rose will become far better known than its namesake.

Clusters of tubular buds unfurl to form rounded semidouble flowers of fuchsia pink. The blooms have a charm I find difficult to convey. They seem to be a refined flower from a Lilliputian land. The long, lime green shoots arch slightly with their own weight, eventually creating an erect bush with great tenacity and vigor. The medium green foliage is rarely touched by blackspot or mildew.

Captain Samuel Holland was a welcome addition to the stable

Hardiness Zone: 3b
Introduced: 1990
Origin: Svejda, Canada
Parentage: L48 × Felix Leclerc
Height: 7 ft. (2 m)
Fragrance: f

of hardy pillar roses that northern gardeners can use as climbers. Its bud hardiness and vigor fall just short of the slightly hardier and more vigorous William Baffin, but not by much.

It is a relatively easy rose to root from softwood cuttings.

Like many of the hardiest climbers, its fragrance is slight at best, but seeing a Captain Samuel Holland in bloom will be payment in full for the planting, fertilizing and pruning efforts you invest.

FELIX LECLERC

Hardiness Zone: 3b (possibly 3a)
Introduced: 2007
Origin: Svejda, Canada
Parentage: (*Rosa kordesii* × (Red Dawn × Suzanne o.p.)) × (Red Dawn × Suzanne o.p.)
Height: 16.5 ft. (5 m)
Fragrance: ff

This rose was selected for testing from a group of seedlings bred by Felicitas Svejda of Agriculture Canada in Ottawa for the Explorer Series of roses. The collection was subsequently moved to L'Assomption, Quebec, where further evaluation and selection took place. We were sent two candidates designated U11 and E18. They were planted in our display garden and grown for two years.

The seedling U11 seemed rather open and sluggish, though the flowers were semidouble and in a lovely deep fuchsia color. The seedling E18 seemed the denser of the two and had similarly colored small flowers in clusters. We were asked to find a name for E18, and so after consultation with a local historian we chose Captain Samuel Holland, a Dutch-born surveyor who did work for the British charting the coasts of what were to become Nova Scotia, Prince Edward Island and New Brunswick. (See page 89.)

Soon afterward, we moved U11 to an easterly facing spot next to the doorway of our office and promptly forgot about it. What happened next became legend at our nursery. By the second year it had grown over 6 ft. (1.75 m) tall, and we decided to build a trellis for it. The third year it reached 10 ft. (3 m) and by the fourth was approaching 16 ft. (5 m) and had topped a second trellis we had built above the first.

While most so-called hardy climbing roses are simply vigorous shrubs, this rose acted more like a vine that sported perhaps five or six upright canes that kept building on the previous year's growth. It is not a plant suitable for open growth, but one that has what most of the world thinks of as a true "climbing rose" look. Its lovely blooms continue until hard frost, and it has a light but pleasant fruity aroma. We felt as if our humble doorway had been transported to one of the great gardens of England.

Though we entreated Agriculture Canada to release U11, we were initially told it was not being considered. Later we offered to buy the rights. This time around we were told it was to be released as Felix Leclerc, part of the new Canadian Artist Series of roses. Someone had taken a second look.

This is our first choice when asked for a climbing rose. It has superb hardiness, a long blooming season and the "look." It also has some of the best resistance to disease we have seen, although be warned that it is loved by leafhoppers. As the plant ages, we cut back one or two old stems each year near the base. This encourages new growth to fill in the base of the plant and provide fresh new shoots for the future.

It roots relatively well, although it is a little slow to take off, so be patient for the first year or two. Felix Leclerc is a "sleeper" in another way. It is a rose that may take a while to find its place in the rose world, but it's also one we think will establish itself as an important cultivar for the north. It will always be on our propagation list, although here at the nursery we still affectionately refer to it as "U11."

GOLDBUSCH

Hardiness Zone: 4a
Introduced: 1954
Origin: Kordes, Germany
Parentage: Golden Glow
   × Obergärtner Wiebicke hybrid
Height: 8 ft. (2.5 m)
Fragrance: fff

Although artists throughout the ages have tried to capture the essence of roses in their works, a bloom from a rose such as Goldbusch relegates all these attempts to the class of pale imitations. We paid very little for our Goldbusch, but this work of art is now among our garden's most cherished possessions.

Goldbusch was bred using the large flowered yellow climber Golden Glow, originally bred by the American breeder Brownell. Goldbusch has inherited that rose's form and vigor. My daughter's plant grows on the south side of her house against a brick wall, and once the long canes reach the eaves she has to turn it downward. Although it will kill back in the coldest winters, this is a good candidate for a climber in Zone 4 and warmer. I have seen this rose rated as a Zone 6 plant. It is definitely hardier than that. In warmer climes it can grow to 20 ft. (6 m).

Even more impressive to me is the healthy glow of the medium green leaves. Although not immune to blackspot, there is little to mar the backdrop they provide for the exquisite blooms.

The tight pyramidal buds are a deep honey color with just a hint of orange. They open into a semidouble flower of alluring soft yellow, a color most rare for a hardy rose. The fragrance is both rich and full bodied, like a well-made Chardonnay wine — a fitting asset of this wonderful flower.

Thankfully, this lovely rose is easy to root from softwood cuttings.

HENRY KELSEY

Hardiness Zone: 4a
Introduced: 1986
Origin: Svejda, Canada
Parentage: *Rosa kordesii* Wulff
   × D24
Height: 8 ft. (2.5 m)
Fragrance: ff

An archway decorated by twining branches clothed in lustrous green foliage and dripping with vivid red roses — Henry Kelsey is the answer to many a northern rose grower's wish.

This Explorer Series introduction from Agriculture Canada has long arching canes that can be tied up and used as a climber, though it might be better classified as a "rambler." If left to grow naturally, Henry Kelsey is a low, arching, pendulous bush. I have used it as a medium-height ground cover, although it is perhaps a bit sparse for this purpose. When tied up, it makes an admirable climber or can be effective when tied horizontally on a fence or trellis. A well-grown Henry Kelsey will send up fantastically vigorous long shoots, which in just a few seasons will top an arch or trellis.

Vigor alone makes Henry Kelsey a standout, but the deep red petals, contrasting with the golden-yellow stamens, create an irresistible lure. Large clusters appear from early summer until the first frosts. The intense red of the new petals gradually fades to a deep rose as the blooms cleanly drop off the bush.

Henry Kelsey is highly resistant to powdery mildew. Although it is not immune to blackspot, this fungal disease is not a serious

threat. We find this rose benefits from some extra feeding. Add a little extra compost or blood meal for a dash of nitrogen and you will be repaid many times over. You can leave this rose on the trellis in Zone 4 without serious winter injury, though we always have a bit of tip damage to prune in the spring. In Zone 5 it is spectacular.

It is easy to propagate from softwood cuttings or layering and will take off even as a young plant.

Henry Kelsey is one of the best bright red climbing roses available for cold areas. It is superior to many existing red climbers, and it should be in every collection where such a rose is desired.

JOHN CABOT

Hardiness Zone: 3b
Introduced: 1978
Origin: Svejda, Canada
Parentage: *Rosa kordesii* Wulff
    × (Masquerade × *Rosa laxa*)
Height: 8 ft. (2.5 m)
Fragrance: ff

Many years ago I walked up to a display of roses at the Agricultural Research Station near us. I was so enthralled by what I saw that I asked permission to take a few cuttings. This was before the days when every new plant was patented. Several roses stood out among the many in the group. One in particular, labeled "L07," caught my eye. The bush was a powerfully upright arching plant covered in symmetrical double blooms that open red, then morph to a deep orchid pink. Its robust healthy glow convinced me that here was a rose worth watching. Several years later I was sent news from Agriculture Canada that a new rose called John Cabot had been released, originally grown as seedling L07.

There is a lovely story that accompanies the history of this rose. The original field where the Explorer Series roses were selected was scheduled to be plowed under. The tractor driver approached Felicitas Svejda, the breeder, and asked that the plant that was later to be named John Cabot be spared, so he could enjoy its blooms. She said yes, and the photo taken of that plant with plowed ground all around it became the photo that was used to promote it.

John Cabot helped to set a new standard for hardy roses.

Its symmetrical, robust form, coupled with its long blooming season and excellent disease resistance, made it one of the most important new roses for northern gardens. It is difficult to know whether to call John Cabot a vigorous shrub rose or a climber, because it can be either. If using it as a climber be warned that it may take some serious pruning to confine the many shoots to a trellis. Since roses with such vigor and long flowering season are rare, I have decided to include it with the climbers.

If you are growing this rose be sure to give it a bit of extra feeding and it will repay you. This seems to be true with many of the *Rosa kordesii* hybrids.

It is reasonably easy to propagate from softwood cuttings, but is slow to take off, so have patience. It will soon dazzle you.

LUCY IRENE

Several years ago we were approached by Jim Nicholson of Fredericton, New Brunswick. He had purchased a William Baffin rose from us several years previously that had been planted at his lakeside cottage. A shoot had appeared beside the William Baffin that appeared identical in all aspects but flower color. This shoot had soft pink flowers, quite different from the deep strawberry pink of the William Baffin.

I made a trip to his cottage and took cuttings from the new shoot. We examined it very carefully and it was definitely a sport, not a seedling. A sport occurs infrequently in plants. It will appear identical in all ways to the original plant, except perhaps with variegated leaves, greater or lesser vigor or, as in this case, a different flower color.

All I could think of was here was a super hardy vigorous pillar rose that could be used as a climber with the color of a rose like New Dawn. Jim decided to call this rose Lucy Irene, after his aunt. Since then we have propagated this rose with the hope that northern rose growers will learn about and plant it. After years of growing Lucy Irene we have never seen a reversion back to the original color, which often happens in sports. This would be called a stable sport. William Baffin is described on page 97, and every characteristic of Lucy Irene will be the same with the

Hardiness Zone: 2b
Introduced: 2012
Origin: Nicholson, Canada
Parentage: color sport of William Baffin
Height: 10 ft. (3 m)
Fragrance: ff

exception of flower color.

Another note of interest is that a similar color sport of William Baffin was discovered by Joe Bergeson of Minnesota. It would be fascinating to compare them.

The origins of roses are usually quite removed and distant from a gardener or propagator. It is exciting to be involved in the dissemination of a new plant with which you are intimately involved.

QUADRA

Hardiness Zone: 3b
Introduced: 1994
Origin: Svejda, Canada
Parentage: B05 ((A15 (Queen
Elizabeth × Arthur Bell) × D35
(Simonet Double Red × Von
Scharnhorst)) × L25 (*Rosa kordesii*
× D07 (Red Dawn × Suzanne)))
Height: 10 ft. (3 m)
Fragrance: ff

I like to think of plants and animals as fragile crystals growing out of the minerals on the Earth's surface into the gases of the atmosphere. Quadra is a rose crystal of exceptional rarity. Hundreds of intense red petals are arranged in a symmetrical pattern reminiscent of the older *gallica* roses, once so common in European gardens. The petals curve, peony-like, toward the center as the rose opens. When the flower expands, these same petals recurve outward, creating a rounded cushion with the texture of soft quilted velvet. While the fragrance is not strong, the bouquet is reminiscent of fresh fruit.

The bush that supports this extravagant arrangement of petals is one of great beauty as well. The new foliage is tinted red. The surface of the older leaves looks freshly polished. A subtle hint of red remains locked within the veins. The bush is vigorous and healthy, and will endure temperatures that would wither red roses of comparable color and form. Quadra forms an upright and somewhat arching shrub that can be trained as a climber. One of the characteristics of this rose is the weak pedicel that supports the blossom. The flowers nod downward. As a shrub this might be seen as a negative feature, but as the plant grows upward the blossoms will look down at you — a definite positive.

The plant is easy to propagate from cuttings, but is a bit slow the first year or so. Have patience and feed it well. It will soon show you that this crystal is deserving of your most special setting.

RAMBLIN' RED

Hardiness Zone: 4b
Introduced: 2002 (by Bailey
Nurseries)
Origin: Radler, USA
Parentage: Razzle Dazzle
× Henry Kelsey
Height: 10 ft. (3 m) in warmer areas
Fragrance: fff

This rose sneaks into our list as a climber because it is a worthy candidate in Zone 5. I might not grow this plant if it were not for the fact that its deep red, superbly fashioned blossoms are irresistible. In our Zone 4 site it does kill back, sometimes severely, but it makes a great shrub. To be fair, I have heard from several gardeners in Zone 4 that their plant has grown to a great height, so perhaps my site is a bit too exposed.

The breeder of this rose, William J. Radler, used the hardy Explorer rose Henry Kelsey to get the hardiness he needed. His floribunda parent provided exquisite form, particularly in the opening bud stage. The flower is quite large and comes in small clusters, repeating some during the rest of the season. It is one of the best hardy roses for arranging, keeping well for several days if picked in the opening bud stage.

It is logical to be conservative about choosing roses, using only those you know will have a good chance at survival, but gardeners, it seems, often save a special place for those that are marginal. Sometimes the thrill of gardening is about testing limits.

This rose is very easy to root and shows great vigor afterward.

THÉRÈSE BUGNET

Hardiness Zone: 2a
Introduced: 1950
Origin: Bugnet, Canada
Parentage: ((*Rosa acicularis*
   × *Rosa kamtchatica*) × (*Rosa*
   amblyotis × *Rosa rugosa plena*))
   × Betty Bland
Height: 10 ft. (3 m)
Fragrance: ￼ffff

There are many unsung plant propagators in far-flung places who never receive the acclamation they deserve. Georges Bugnet of Legal, Alberta, is such a person. Emigrating from his native France in 1905, Bugnet arrived in a land with rich soil but intensely cold winters. Roses had to withstand temperatures that regularly fell to −40°F (−40°C) or colder. Using the native roses, as well as roses he imported from such exotic places as the Kamchatka Peninsula in the Soviet Union, Bugnet created some of the hardiest garden roses in existence. One in particular is a rose of uncommon distinction — Thérèse Bugnet.

This is a remarkable rose not only for its unusual hardiness, but also for the large and intensely fragrant blossoms that occur so prolifically from late spring to early fall. When this impressive, fountain-like bush first blooms, the foliage is barely visible. Later flushes are less showy, but it is rarely out of bloom during the season. The tissue-paper texture of this soft pink rose has an informal look, yet the plant has lost the wild look of its parents and is sophisticated enough for virtually any garden.

Thérèse Bugnet also gives color to the landscape in winter. The well-balanced arching stems of this vigorous bush are a deep clear red. These same stems have the added advantage of being nearly prickle free near the flowers, making them much easier to pick for bouquets than many of the shrub roses.

This rose is extremely easy to root from softwood cuttings. As the plant ages, thin out the oldest canes, which will be deep gray. Leave a hand's width above the ground and deep red new shoots will emerge along the stub, renewing the bush with new deep red stems.

WILLIAM BAFFIN

Hardiness Zone: 2b
Introduced: 1983
Origin: Svejda, Canada
Parentage: L48 (*Rosa kordesii*
Wulff × D15) o.p.
Height: 10 ft. (3 m)
Fragrance: ff

One of my favorite pastimes is watching how people react when they walk through the gate of our garden and look out across the multitude of shrubs, perennials, vines and evergreens that lies before them. In the late summer, as many of the roses and day-lilies are waning, most eyes are instantly drawn to a corner where a semicircular hedge of robust rosebushes grows.

William Baffin has impressed us, not only with its strawberry ice cream flowers, but also with its vigor and health. As a bush, William Baffin is upright and slightly arching, with a dense, full look — perfect for a tall informal hedge. Using it as a climber, your only problem may be keeping its vigor from overfilling the trellis with strong, thick canes. You certainly will not have to worry about fussing over this rose. Unless your winter is truly arctic, you will be able to grow William Baffin.

We have never seen an injured bud in our garden. It is very healthy — not suffering from blackspot, mildew or rust — but is somewhat susceptible to *Cercospora rosicola*, also called frog eye. However, don't let this deter you from obtaining this tough rose. Be sure to feed it well. An underfed specimen will not have the bright green foliage you expect.

It is relatively easy to root from softwood cuttings, although the rooting is a bit sparse. Once in the ground it will take off.

The loose, carefree blooms of William Baffin are charming.

They are certainly not aristocratic. If you are looking for a healthy, ironclad hardy, robust rose that is blanketed by clusters of bloom throughout the entire season, this is the rose for you.

7 TALL SHRUBS

Shrubs growing to 7 ft. (2 m) or more

◄ The aptly named Robusta,
whose single blooms are the
most intense of reds, can
reach a height of 8 ft. (2.5 m).

ALBA MAXIMA

Hardiness Zone: 3b
Introduced: ca. 1400
Origin: Europe
Parentage: unknown, possibly a
Rosa alba mutation
Height: 8 ft. (2.5 m)
Fragrance: ffff

Years ago, I was driving through a quiet Nova Scotia fishing village marveling at a landscape that looked as though a pair of giants had tired of their game of marbles, dropped their room-sized granite aggies and gone home. In front of a quaint old house with green shutters I spied an immense arching rosebush that looked as if it had been growing there since the marble game had ended.

It was covered in large, creamy double blooms and had the most handsome gray-green foliage imaginable. This was my introduction to Alba Maxima.

Once called the Jacobite Rose or the Great White Rose, this cultivar was very popular in 16th-century Europe and was used as the emblem of the Jacobites, who supported Bonnie Prince Charlie of the House of Stuart. It has proven its historical longevity and, as testified by its windy home among the seaside granite boulders, its hardiness.

Give this rosebush plenty of room. It will grow quite tall but requires little in the way of pruning, except to thin the canes here and there. Although there are some prickles, the shoots are fairly smooth. Walking up to this bush and inhaling the fragrance of its blooms is a great way to celebrate the warmth of a new summer. In winter it will provide a colorful display of orange-red hips.

We find about half of our cuttings will root if taken just as flower buds open.

ALBA SEMI-PLENA

Hardiness Zone: 3b
Introduced: ca. 1620–30
Origin: unknown, Europe
Parentage: considered a sport of
Alba Maxima
Height: 8 ft. (2.5 m)
Fragrance: fff

A sport that occurs on a rose is usually propagated because it has more petals than the original. In this case Alba Semi-Plena, also known as the White Rose of York, is a sport that has fewer petals than its original Alba Maxima form. The result is a pristine white semi-double with a large central boss of golden yellow stamens. The fact that it has fewer petals changes the feel of the rose, giving it what might be called a more relaxed feel than the very full Alba Maxima. The bush becomes a large plant with gracefully arching stems that turn a gray-green color. The prickles are scattered along the stems and are decorative in their own right. The red hips add colorful accents to the garden in the fall and will eventually feed the birds.

This rose is quite hardy and worth trying in most northern gardens. It makes a great backdrop for a large bed or where a large specimen is desired. It is a rose that will grow on you as it grows into a mature plant. Keep your pruning to an absolute minimum. Because it is not overly dense, and the blossoms only form on the previous year's growth, pruning back will lessen the rose's impact. If pruning is necessary, do so just after the bloom finishes.

Like Alba Maxima, Semi-Plena is not as easy to root as most. If cuttings are taken just as flowering commences, you will have around a 50 to 60 percent success rate.

ALEXANDER MACKENZIE

Hardiness Zone: 3b
Introduced: 1985
Origin: Svejda, Canada
Parentage: Queen Elizabeth
    × (Red Dawn × Suzanne o.p.)
Height: 8 ft. (2.5 m)
Fragrance: fff

Alexander Mackenzie is a well-tailored rose. Its foliage and form create an elegant backdrop for the flowers, which embroider the bush more skillfully than any tailor's threads might. The bush is upright and symmetrically arching. I could have just as easily placed this rose with the climbers. I once saw an astounding specimen in Michigan that had reached heights mine have never equalled.

The tall tulip-like deep raspberry buds open to reveal a classic form with delicately folded petals curling back as the first warm days of summer draw them out. The petals gradually mellow to a deep, warm pink. As if true to their color, the flowers exude the fragrance of fresh-picked raspberries; however, it is interesting to note that about one-third of the people we have offered a blossom to smell say they detect nothing. Pity.

On our hillside the roses have three successive waves of bloom during the season, the last flowers fading in September's first light frosts. After a wet period you will sometimes find the exterior petals browning, and the odd imperfect petal may appear at the flower's base. Aside from a few stray petals, Alexander Mackenzie is a most gratifying rose to grow.

The most welcome news is that

this rose is a remarkably hardy plant. It has impressive resistance to disease, although it does attract leafhoppers and sawflies. The leaves have a waxy sheen that exudes health. The deep reddish new foliage is an added extra of this extraordinary rose, complementing the dark green of the older leaves. This is another rose that benefits from a little pampering with extra compost or nitrogen-rich amendments.

It can be propagated easily from softwood cuttings.

If I told you I know of a rose that is hardy, healthy, beautiful and fragrant, wouldn't you be tempted?

BELLE AMOUR

If love has a fragrance it would resemble the scent of this rose. Belle Amour has the aroma of myrrh, and we can never get enough. The perfume comes from a semidouble, coral-pink cupped flower of great beauty growing on a vigorous upright plant that is well armed against those who would wish it harm.

This could have been a chance seeding, but was more likely an older rose that was a either a local cultivar or one that had fallen into near oblivion. It was rediscovered by Lady Nancy Lindsay in France and introduced back into the world

Hardiness Zone: 3b
Introduced: before 1940
Origin: found by Lindsay (UK), France
Parentage: unknown, *Rosa alba*, possibly with *Rosa damascena*
Height: 7 ft. (2 m)
Fragrance: fff

of roses. She was no doubt as enchanted as we are with this unique rose. It is one we always look forward to, and it keeps us waiting — it comes into bloom later than most.

Taken early in the flowering season, it will root easily.

BLANC DOUBLE DE COUBERT

Hardiness Zone: 2b
Introduced: 1892
Origin: Cochet-Cochet, France
Parentage: *Rosa rugosa* × Sombreuil
Height: 7 ft. (2 m)
Fragrance: ffff

This large white rose is one of the first that comes to mind when we think of fragrance. Like wines, roses have their degrees of sweetness. Blanc is definitely a sweet port, with a fragrance so strong you can actually overdose by inhaling deeply inside a freshly opening blossom.

The loosely arranged petals, clustered around their yellow centers, reflect the wayward, vigorous shoots of this bush. Over time they form impressive speci-

mens, or in groups, large informal hedges. The first flush of bloom resembles an immense swarm of large, pure white butterflies resting on the deep green foliage and is a sight even for eyes jaded by the many competing flowers of spring. The blooms continue to appear until the nights get their first real chill. Although not as numerous later in the season, Blanc's blooms always have a perfumed treat for the garden wanderer.

If you are in search of a delicate, well-mannered rose, look elsewhere. Blanc is a robust grower and a thicket-type bush, sending suckers outward as it grows. This very vigor makes Blanc a valuable plant for stabilizing steep banks or creating hedges and large beds.

Unless you live where winter temperatures can freeze spit before it hits the ground, you stand a chance of overwintering Blanc. This adaptable and healthy rose is one of the most important of the truly hardy roses, and it is often cited as the purest white rose of all.

Softwood cuttings root relatively easily if taken early in the season just as flowering commences, and suckers can be used.

CANADIAN SHIELD

Hardiness Zone: 3a
Introduced: 2017
Origin: Dyck, Canada
Parentage: RSMY8 × Frontenac
Height: 7 ft. (2 m)
Fragrance: f

Every rose has a history. This one began in 2001 with the dusting of pollen from an older floriferous Explorer rose called Frontenac onto the ripe pistil of a promising seedling labeled RSMY8. The man doing the dusting was a tireless employee of the Morden Research and Development Centre in Manitoba. Larry Dyck was employed as a technician, and his hands and eyes have been, in many ways, responsible for a great many important roses. Though he would no doubt deny the title, for many he is an unsung hero of rose breeding. The result of this cross was planted in the observation field and named according to its place in the row and its parents: 21Y8FR04.

It grew for many years in the field before being selected and renamed AAC 576. Its remarkable assets were remarked on by many, and these positive comments eventually led it to be selected as the first introduction in a new series of roses launched by the Vineland Research and Innovation Centre in Ontario called the 49th Parallel Series.

Canadian Shield has proven outstanding. Its petals are deep red with slightly lighter undersides. The flowers are born individually on thin stems or in small clusters. Unlike many red roses, these do not fade. They stay brilliant and are presented against a foil of glossy green leaves that are tinged red and show virtually no disease, even into the fall. Best of all, for those in northern climes this plant is exceptionally hardy with great vigor as well. The plant is exceedingly easy to root, and its vigor becomes quickly evident.

Though relatively new in the rose world, Canadian Shield has surpassed all other reds in my opinion and will be an important milestone in the continually evolving history of roses. We will see much of this newcomer. Such is the pleasure of new arrivals.

CARMENETTA

Hardiness Zone: 2b
Introduced: 1923
Origin: Preston, Canada
Parentage: *Rosa glauca* (formerly *Rosa rubrifolia*) × *Rosa rugosa*
Height: 13 ft. (4 m)
Fragrance: f

If I lived in a place where there are only 50 frost-free days a year, and where winter temperatures routinely plummet to −40°F (−40°C) or colder, I would be limited to a small selection of the very hardiest roses. Carmenetta would probably be one of them.

Carmenetta is a seedling of the Red Leafed Rose (*Rosa glauca*), a species with a lovely arching form and reddish foliage that gives the plant a warm glow, even when not covered by its star-shaped single pink blooms. The breeder, Isabella Preston, gently dusted pollen from a *Rosa rugosa* onto the centers of the flowers of her Red Leafed Rose. Each seed was carefully saved, planted and observed as it grew. After several years one seedling in particular caught her eye most often. It was a robust arching plant with flowers that were noticeably larger than those of its siblings. Nearly 100 years later I grow this same seedling in my garden, and so can you.

The red pigments that run all through this rose also color its bark, so that the deep red new growth colorfully accents the graceful silhouette of Carmenetta in the snow. Those pigments also suffuse the veins of each flower petal, making the entire plant an enormous pink bouquet.

If there is a warning, or for some an enticement, this plant grows to an immense size with stems that become tree-like. It will need a large space if you allow it to attain maturity. But if you want to keep it more contained, bring out the loppers.

Carmenetta is relatively easy to propagate from softwood cuttings. The plant's fruit is oval and reddish-purple.

Like a first romance, Carmenetta does not last as long as we wish, but the experience is enough to make us long for our next affair.

CHLORIS

Hardiness Zone: 4a (possibly 3b)
Introduced: before 1848
Origin: Descemet, France
Parentage: unknown, *Rosa alba* hybrid
Height: 8 ft. (2.5 m)
Fragrance: ffff

The search for roses with no prickles has a long history, and even today the goal of a first-class prickle-free rose occupies many a breeder. Some are available to growers. The most famous is the Bourbon rose Zéphirine Drouhin. While hardy by most standards, this rose is not tough enough for the coldest areas. There is a rose, however, that is virtually free of prickles, exceptionally hardy and exceedingly beautiful. Its name is Chloris.

Chloris is a translucent, diaphanous pink. Its numerous reflexed petals are arranged around a neat central button. It is a large and striking flower that is called by some Rosée du Matin (dew in the morning).

The scent of the soft, double blooms is exquisite and something that I will always go out of my way to smell. These large perfumed powder puffs bloom for around six weeks, as do most of the *Rosa alba* group, although some have reported the odd flower later in the season.

The plant is quite vigorous, with long, green arching stems that look as good after a bitter cold winter as they did when the first snow bedded them down. The foliage is deepest green and a picture of health, giving the plant presence even when not in bloom. On top of this, when you go to collect a fresh spray of flowers for your table, the beast will not bite.

We find Chloris relatively easy to root.

DAVID THOMPSON

Hardiness Zone: 3a
Introduced: 1979
Origin: Svejda, Canada
Parentage: (Schneezwerg
  × Frü Dagmar Hastrup) o.p.
Height: 7 ft. (2 m)
Fragrance: fff

Roses can be grown for their lovely flowers, for their productivity or for their usefulness in the landscape. David Thompson fills all these slots. Plus — and this is an important plus — it is never out of bloom once it commences. After the first magnificent flush, flowers can always be found on this bush, as if it's trying to keep your interest until the next substantial wave of bloom begins.

The bush eventually becomes sizable and dense, making it ideal for an imposing informal hedge. Its medium green foliage has a quality that makes it easy to pick out from a distance.

The flowers are enchanting upon close inspection. In early morning you can see the buds open to a cupped blossom that flattens its many petals as they expand, their color on the pink spectrum of mauve. In the center you will usually see a petal or two with a narrow streak of white, a good identification clue.

This rose has had little fanfare over the years and is somewhat more difficult to find than others. Like all the roses introduced by Felicitas Svejda when she worked for Agriculture Canada, they stand up to the test of time. This rose never lets us down. It is relatively easy to root. It never has disease. The only insect damage noticeable is the odd flower distorted by thrips, and this is rarely an issue later in the season. Every part of this plant is solid and delivers its promise.

EMILY CARR

Hardiness Zone: 3b
Introduced: 2007
Origin: Collicutt, Canada
Parentage: ((Lammert's
    Selection × Morden Cardinette)
    × Morden Cardinette)
    × Cuthbert Grant
Height: 7 ft. (2 m)
Fragrance: f

Deep red tulips come to mind when I see the buds of this rose unfurl. The blooms are high centered, rich red semidouble flowers that come in waves throughout the season.

Although I initially thought this rose would prove to be a low and somewhat tender rose, I was pleasantly surprised to be wrong. Bushes planted for a few years have pushed their near vertical stems upward to a substantial height. This column of dark green stems has foliage rarely blemished by disease and is continually decorated by its shapely blooms. You may see thrips distorting the petals early in the season, though these later disappear. Emily Carr is also relatively easy to root.

This is another release from Agriculture Canada's Canadian Artist Series. It was bred at the Morden Research and Development Centre in Manitoba using Cuthbert Grant, a very large deep red rose and a seedling bred from a long line of Morden roses such as Morden Cardinette, Assiniboine, Adelaide Hoodless and others. Both Cuthbert Grant and the seedling have a lineage that began with a cross using *Rosa arkansana*, a rose that contrib- uted its extreme hardiness. It can be argued that Emily Carr contains the best attributes of all its ancestors.

Emily Carr was a bold and imaginative artist who spent much of her career painting the Pacific coast of British Columbia and helped bring the wonders of the Indigenous culture of Haida Gwaii to the attention of the world. This rose is a suitable testament to her life and work. I think she would be pleased.

F.J. GROOTENDORST

Hardiness Zone: 3b
Introduced: 1918 (possibly ca. 1908–10)
Origin: attributed to De Goey, Netherlands (but more likely Skinner, Canada)
Parentage: *Rosa rugosa* × Mme. Norbert Levavasseur
Height: 7 ft. (2 m)
Fragrance: f

F.J. Grootendorst has a prolific display of small, soft red flowers, more reminiscent of carnations than roses. The flowers appear in large clusters. Its long season, hardiness and dangerously well-armed thrusting canes covered in deep green foliage have ensured it a place in the northern garden. Indeed this is one of the few truly continuous bloomers. Once in bloom it is never without flowers until frost.

This rose has also become an intriguing mystery. It has been assumed that F.J. Grootendorst was created by a Dr. De Goey of

the Netherlands and introduced by Grootendorst Nurseries of Holland in 1918. However, in my research I found these lines in *Horticultural Horizons: Plant Breeding and Introduction at Dropmore, Manitoba* by Canadian breeder Frank Leith Skinner.

"My first attempt at plant breeding was with roses. Either in 1907 or 1908 I crossed *Rosa rugosa* with one of our wild roses and this success encouraged me to try some other crosses. I used pollen of Mme. Norbert Levavasseur on *Rosa rugosa* and obtained three seedlings, one of which was identical with the variety that was to be brought out about fifteen years later as F.J. Grootendorst. It was not, however, entirely hardy, usually killing back to within a foot of the ground each winter, although it did flower quite freely on the wood that survived.

"I rather liked this rose and thinking it might do well at Ottawa I dug it up, together with some other plants and sent them on to Dr. W.T. Macoun at the Central Experimental Farm, Ottawa. The same day I also sent some plants to Professor F.W. Brodrick at the Manitoba Agricultural College. Both parcels were sent by the same railway from Roblin; no parcel reached Professor Brodrick, and the plants which he should have received were delivered to Dr. Macoun. It was too late by this time to bother about the parcel that had disappeared.

"I wrote to F.J. Grootendorst, Boskoop, Holland, after I had seen the Grootendorst rose and asked if he would care to let me know its parentage as I too was

engaged in breeding roses and other plants suitable for our climate. In his reply he stated that his firm had bought the rose with the privilege of naming it, and that it was a chance seedling that had appeared among a batch of rugosa seedlings raised by a small grower near Boskoop. Since then I have seen it listed as having been raised in 1918 by Dr. Goey, the result of a cross between *Rosa rugosa* and Mme. Norbert Levavasseur. Mr. Herman Grootendorst told me that they had had this rose before 1914 but had been unable to market it owing to the war. There is, apparently, some doubt as to who did propagate the rose known as F.J. Grootendorst. I definitely raised an identical rose and its parentage was *Rosa rugosa* × Mme. Norbert Levavasseur."

A great story. I will let the historians find the truth. Whatever the verdict, F.J. Grootendorst will remain famous for its beauty and toughness.

Since its introduction, several color sports have appeared. Grootendorst Supreme is a deeper red with somewhat more vigor and deeper green foliage. It flowers slightly later than the other sports. Pink Grootendorst is a soft flesh-pink sport, and White Grootendorst is a white-flowered sport of Pink Grootendorst that sometimes reverts to the pink color. There are even instances where individual flowers will have half-pink, half-white coloration.

Grootendorst roses root fairly easily. We find cuttings from the smaller diameter lateral branches yield better results than using the thicker vigorous canes.

FRÜHLINGSGOLD

Hardiness Zone: 4a
Introduced: 1937
Origin: Kordes, Germany
Parentage: Joanna Hill
    × *Rosa spinosissima* L.
Height: 7.5 ft. (2.25 m)
Fragrance: ff

I was once given a bundle of root pieces from a Harison's Yellow rose by a generous and dynamic 90-year-old lady, who was also a first-class gardener. When the plants began blooming I noticed one was quite different. Although yellow, it was a larger and slightly paler rose with fewer petals. For many years this orphan remained a mystery to me. Then one day, while reading through Peter Beale's *Classic Roses*, I saw a picture of Frühlingsgold and knew immediately it was my mystery rose.

True to its name, Frühlingsgold, which translates as "spring gold," helps to usher in the rose season. Its large semidouble blooms are an ethereal primrose yellow. Our type of soil adds mysterious shadings of pale pink, giving the barest hint of an accent to this soft pastel flower.

The bush is a strong and resourceful plant. As this rose matures, the branches create a pattern of numerous intersecting arcs, a silhouette that remains airy, not dense. The stems reflect their flower's color; the green of the new growth is suffused with goldenrod yellow until time fades them to gray. The bases of the stems are cloaked in small reddish-yellow prickles. The leaves have edges that fold under, giving the foliage a soft look that becomes a quilted backdrop for the flowers. Though generally healthy, a damp spring can initiate some blackspot, so preventative measures might be in order. We never spray, and our plants stay in good condition most years.

Frühlingsgold is most often budded or grafted. It can be difficult to root. Use vigorous wood that is free of disease. Take your cuttings just as it is setting flower buds. Maintain a high humidity, but do not keep the cuttings wet. When roots appear, transplant as gently as possible into a good growing medium.

In the garden this rose exhibits uncommon hardiness, and the tips seldom suffer from frostbite. It seems to succeed even in rather poor, dry soils, although with care and good soil you can grow blooms whose delicate pastels will undoubtedly enroll you as a new member of the Frühlingsgold fan club.

GERANIUM

Startling might be an appropriate adjective for this plant. It would be difficult to imagine a brighter red than that possessed by this single rose. It is a shade reminiscent of Chinese red lacquer. Although blooming for only a few weeks in early summer, it deserves a space in your garden, where its long, gracefully arching stems can have their place in the sun. The triangular prickles that grow evenly spaced along the ascending shoots are quite ornamental, particularly in winter. Another endearing winter feature is the profusion of bright red hips, shaped like ancient amphorae.

The leaves are small and delicate, but plentiful enough to

Hardiness Zone: 4b
Introduced: 1938
Origin: Mulligan, UK
Parentage: *Rosa moyesii* seedling
Height: 8 ft. (2.5 m)
Fragrance: f

adequately clothe its bones. If you live where temperatures do not fall below –13°F (–25°C), try to locate Eddies Jewel. It is a repeat blooming version of this rose.

Geranium is a bit difficult to root. Collect your cuttings just as the flower buds form and do not keep them too wet or they will drop their leaves. This is a good candidate for a cold frame.

HANSA

Venerable bushes of Hansa grow on innumerable old farm sites throughout the countryside where I live. In the suburbs, younger plants have appeared, taken there by the sons and daughters of those who first planted these roses. This was also a pioneer rose in the Prairie provinces of Canada, where most roses perished after their first winter. For many, this cultivar represents the term "hardy rose."

These long-lived plants form immense mounds, often hollow on the inside from lack of light. The large mauve-red flowers bloom until late summer. Hansa is generally very healthy with no serious insect problems. Its beauty, tenacity, hardiness and ease of propagation have made the plant common, the highest compliment in horticulture.

One of the most enduring appeals of Hansa is the heady draft of fragrance on a still summer evening. Although you can eat the petals, those after more substance will delight in chewing around the core of a Hansa rose hip. This

Hardiness Zone: 2b
Introduced: 1905
Origin: Schaum and Van Tol, Netherlands
Parentage: *Rosa rugosa* hybrid
Height: 7.5 ft. (2.25 m)
Fragrance: fff

rose produces a profusion of deep orange-red fruits that are large and meaty — just right for the makers of rose hip tea, those who cherish late autumn color or birds.

There are several new cultivars of *Rosa rugosa* that are similar to Hansa with perhaps better flower production and a longer season, but Hansa will always hold a cherished place in the history of hardy roses.

HARISON'S SALMON

Hardiness Zone: 3a
Introduced: 1929
Origin: Hamblin, USA
Parentage: Harison's Yellow o.p.
Height: 7.5 ft. (2.25 m)
Fragrance: ff

This is not a rose most would include in a book on roses. It is a spreader, though the same can be said of many great roses. Many lovely gallica roses such as Tuscany and Charles de Mills are spreaders, a negative attribute if you are planting in a small space, but there is a need for plants that spread and form interwoven networks of roots that can stabilize ground such as slopes or areas where erosion control is needed.

However, you don't need a steep slope to grow this rather rare rose. Those with enough space will find it a fantastic filler. The bush is very dense with medium green foliage and a color that is uncommon among all roses. The petals on this semidouble flower are primrose yellow with subtle infusions of salmon pink toward their centers, especially in cool weather. The blooms are cupped and form pastel sprays that are quite enchanting. Though it blooms but a few weeks, the bush makes up for it with a copious display in those weeks, enough to satisfy you until they return at the next summer solstice.

This rose appears to have been named with the hope that using part of the name of a well-known rose, in this case its parent plant Harison's Yellow, would attract attention and encourage growers and gardeners to try it.

HARISON'S YELLOW

Hardiness Zone: 3a
Introduced: 1825
Origin: Harison, USA
Parentage: *Rosa foetida*
   × *Rosa spinosissima* L.
Height: 7 ft. (2 m)
Fragrance: ff

Very little is known about the creator of this world-famous rose. His name was George Folliott Harison. We know he was a lawyer who lived in Manhattan, New York City, but otherwise few details have been uncovered.

It is assumed that sometime in the late 1700s or early 1800s Harison began growing roses. There are at least two possibilities for this rose's origin that seem likely. Either the rose was a chance seedling Harison found in his garden or Harison performed a controlled cross and this was a result. It is doubtful we will ever know the full story, but the thought of this man sitting on a stool at the turn of a bygone century dusting the pollen of a Scotch rose onto the pistil of his *Rosa foetida* has me hoping for the latter possibility. So many great things come from one person's passion. Harison's good luck is still creating spring mounds of dazzling yellow in gardens around the world.

It has been claimed that one of the parents of Harison's Yellow is the Persian Yellow, a double form of *Rosa foetida*. However, this rose was not introduced into America until 1838, after Harison had introduced his creation. It is therefore believed the parent that gave the rose its color was a single form of *Rosa foetida*, the species from which Persian Yellow arose. One has to wonder where the genes for a doubling of the petals comes from. The other parent might have been a double form of the Scotch rose (*Rosa spinosissima*), a very hardy parent that appears to have bequeathed the rose with a better resistance to blackspot, a disease that haunts *foetida*.

Whatever the circumstances of its birth, Harison's Yellow shot to fame as the first double deep yellow rose to appear in the Americas. It soon traveled across the continent and made its way north as well, for this was a very hardy rose. The name "Yellow Rose of Texas" has often been assigned to this rose; however, the song of the same name, created some time in the 1830s, actually refers to a woman, not a rose.

Whether in the scorching heat of a Texas summer or in the deep freeze of a northern winter, this adaptable rose has earned a place in the hearts of many.

Harison's Yellow is an early bloomer, like its parents. The numerous small buds turn themselves inside out to reveal the sulfur yellow petals hidden within. The delicate branches of this unassuming shrub suddenly become arching sprays of sunshine. This tropical display lasts but a few weeks and we are left with a rather coarse and humble bush for the remainder of the season; but, like the sun, Harison's Yellow can't shine forever, and if it did, we would not appreciate its radiance as much.

If someone can find a way to root cuttings of this rose, I want to talk to them. We have tried many times with virtually no success. We once took nearly a thousand cuttings and ended up with four weakly rooted plants. It is nearly always budded; however, suckers can be used and they are the primary way it has been spread over continents through the centuries.

HAZELDEAN

Hardiness Zone: 2a
Introduced: 1948
Origin: Wright, Canada
Parentage: *Rosa spinosissima altaica* × Persian Yellow
Height: 7 ft. (2 m) or more
Fragrance: fff

If you love yellow but live where temperatures dip below the −40°F (−40°C) mark with regularity, this is the rose for you. I think it is safe to say that Hazeldean is the hardiest deep yellow rose ever created.

We owe thanks to its creator Percy Wright of Saskatchewan. Wright was a man of many talents, but horticulture was his passion. He started a fruit tree nursery, but this undertaking was eventually abandoned. Later he spent whatever free time he had breeding roses. Of the thousands of seedlings he raised it was Hazeldean he considered his "greatest triumph."

Harry McGee, in his carefully researched book *The Rosemakers*, notes that there was some confusion about the yellow parent of Hazeldean. Initially it was believed the pollen parent was Harison's Yellow, but in his correspondence with Walter Schowalter, Wright said the pollen was derived from buds of Persian Yellow that were sent to him.

Although far more resistant to blackspot than Persian Yellow, Hazeldean is affected by this disease, but not to the extent that it usually defoliates. In drier areas this is not a problem. Another fault is a propensity for the flowers to ball in wet weather. If heavy rains hit during peak flowering most will not open. Even so, Hazeldean puts on a fantastic show of bright yellow blossoms that lasts for at least a month when conditions are right. This rose shines in the northern parts of Canada's Prairie provinces, where sunlight is more likely than rain.

This rose is challenging to root. Take cuttings just at flower initiation and avoid misting too heavily. We are usually able to root about 50 percent of our cuttings.

JENS MUNK

Hardiness Zone: 2b
Introduced: 1979
Origin: Svejda, Canada
Parentage: Schneezwerg
   × Frü Dagmar Hastrup
Height: 7.5 ft. (2.25 m)
Fragrance: fff

If I had to pick the pinkest of the *Rosa rugosa* hybrids this rose would be at the top of the list. It gets its pink from Frü Dagmar Hastrup, which is a silvery pink single. This rose, however, is a deep pink double that, unlike both its parents, is a vigorous, upright, tall plant.

Of course the gardener has access to pruning shears and can keep Jens Munk to any size they want. We have found it an excellent hedging plant, particularly if you want to keep people out. It has some of the most wicked prickles of any rose I know. The workers jokingly refer to it as Jens Junk. Messing with this plant without good leather gloves is akin to masochism. It makes up for this armature with excellent flower production throughout the season as well as good fragrance. It is also a plant whose foliage will almost never show a spot of disease. It has performed better than nearly every other rose in its class.

Jens Munk is one of the first roses released in the Explorer Series from Agriculture Canada, named after an explorer who was born in Norway, then moved to Denmark when he was eight. He fought for the Danish king and later explored the coasts of Greenland and Hudson Bay in the Canadian Arctic in search of the Northwest Passage to India. Though not successful in this quest, his namesake rose is a testament to his legacy.

JOHN DAVIS

Hardiness Zone: 3a
Introduced: 1986
Origin: Svejda, Canada
Parentage: *Rosa kordesii*
　× (Red Dawn × Suzanne o.p.)
Height: up to 7.5 ft. (2.25 m) if
　trained
Fragrance: ff

When they unfold, the semidouble blooms of John Davis flatten their outside petals, as if presenting their camellia-shaped centers of folded petals to the viewer. Gradually the centers continue unfolding until the blossoms lie open. They are pink — the pinkest of pinks. If I had to choose one shade of pink to represent the color, it would be this shade. There are no hints of red or orange or purple. It is not a deep pink, nor a light pink. Just a pink.

The bush is vigorous but somewhat sprawling, looking almost like a many-legged creature trying to walk away from where it is anchored. Those legs are slender, smooth and deep red. It eventually becomes a large, lax shrub.

Many have used this rose as a medium-sized climber. You will need to tie up the canes to create height; however, your efforts will be rewarded with a wall of pink in late spring and a quilt sprinkled with a pink floral pattern through summer and fall.

This is among the hardiest of roses. Our specimens have never experienced any winter injury — not a bud. It is a rose well prepared for the far north. As with so many of the Explorer Series roses, it is also highly disease resistant, although it does attract leafhoppers and sawflies early in the season.

Take your cuttings as the first roses appear. It is not a difficult rose to root. Just make sure you place your new plant into an enriched soil. We have found Mr. Davis needs that extra bit of nutrition to make his foliage deep green and his flowers plentiful.

LAVENDER BOUQUET

Hardiness Zone: 4a (possibly 3b)
Introduced: 2019
Origin: MacPhail, Canada
Parentage: Apple Blossom (*Rosa
　multiflora* hybrid) × seedling
Height: 7.5 ft. (2.25 m)
Fragrance: f

It is a rare event to be witness to the introduction of a new rose. This is one of many seedlings bred by the Nova Scotian rosarian George MacPhail that we were given to test. Several were excellent roses, but the winter of 2016–17 killed most of them

back to the crown. The one that stood tall and undeterred was this rose. The original name, Lavender Lady, had to be abandoned, as there was already a rose with this name. Lavender Bouquet was suggested, as these lovely lavender flowers arrive in very large and dense clusters.

The bush is extremely vigorous with long arching canes that are grass green with few prickles. This habit would be useful to those who wish to create a climbing rose, although it is rather dense for that purpose. As a specimen it is spectacular. The individual flowers

are small, but the immense clusters create a sensational display.

You may get some repeat later in the season. It roots very easily.

LOUISE BUGNET

Hardiness Zone: 2b
Introduced: before 1960
Origin: Bugnet, Canada
Parentage: Martha Bugnet
   × Thérèse Bugnet
Height: 7 ft. (2 m)
Fragrance: fff

There are a few special people who make it their life's passion to find and collect rare roses. Such a person is Margit Schowalter, the daughter of Walter Schowalter, a rose breeder who worked in Alberta in the 20th century. Margit started collecting all the roses her father had bred, then branched out to find as many of the rapidly disappearing roses created by breeders in Alberta, Saskatchewan and Manitoba as she could. Once collected, she would grow the cuttings or suckers she obtained and then pass cuttings on to others, so that their legacy could continue. We were one of the beneficiaries of her dedication and are now growing many of these rare plants.

Among the finest of these once endangered roses is Louise Bugnet, bred by Georges Bugnet, the same man who created the better known Thérèse Bugnet, now grown throughout the world. He produced many roses, all of them fine, extremely hardy selections and nearly all named after his family members. Interestingly, Bugnet was not interested in self-promotion, and it fell to others to introduce his roses.

Louise Bugnet stands out in many ways. The bush is very vigorous and absolutely hardy into Zone 2. The foliage is completely clean. The stems are nearly without prickles. The flower buds are a charming combination of white with purple striping. When open, the very double pure white blooms rival such icons as Blanc Double de Coubert, although perhaps with a subtle shift toward ivory. In addition, the plant's marvelous flowers continue to appear even into fall. Very few of the heritage roses can boast such a long season.

We try to collect our cuttings at the beginning of flowering for best results. We usually have good crops and hope to increase our production of this valuable rose. It is such a wonderful feeling to be creating fine plants that once stood on the edge of extinction.

MAIDEN'S BLUSH

Hardiness Zone: 4a
Introduced: ca. 1400
Origin: unknown
Parentage: unknown, *Rosa alba* group
Height: 7 ft. (2 m)
Fragrance: ffff

There are actually two forms of this popular rose. The most common form is Great Maiden's Blush, and the less common is Small Maiden's Blush. The only difference between the two is the comparative size of the bush and flower. Whichever form, it is difficult to find a rose that creates more response from people than Maiden's Blush. That this rose is still popular after 600 years is a testament to its immense appeal. It is a rose with an intoxicating aroma, sensuous color and perfection of form.

The bush is a tall grower with stiffly erect stems and blue-tinted foliage that sometimes shows a bit of blackspot, but is otherwise healthy and abundant. Like so many of its *Rosa alba* kin, Maiden's Blush is very hardy. In early summer sweetly scented blossoms of warmest blush pink arrive in great numbers. A good deal of this rose's charm is due to the informally arranged and gently folded petals which, although neatly contained, have an endearing character that must be seen to be appreciated. When the Maiden's Blush comes into bloom, the rose season becomes complete for us.

This rose, aptly and more sensuously named Cuisse de Nymph (nymph's thighs) in France, will continue to be one of the most popular of the older shrub roses. For me the only disappointment is that it never lasts long enough.

Maiden's Blush is generally budded or grafted, although it is fairly easy to root if cuttings are taken just as flowering begins. Be sure to use material that is free of any disease.

MME. PLANTIER

Hardiness Zone: 4a
Introduced: 1835
Origin: Plantier, France
Parentage: *Rosa damascena* Mill. × *Rosa moschata* Herrm.
Height: 10 ft. (3 m)
Fragrance: ffff

As you gaze out your window through the crystals of snow settling on the leafless form of your rosebushes, your eyes are drawn to a fountain of arching grass-green stems. These nearly prickle-free stems belong to one of the most famous of the *Rosa alba* group of hybrids, Mme. Plantier, which is sometimes classified as a Damask rose. This robust grower will survive the frigid winter, and next summer those same bright green stems will be weighed down with hundreds of pure white quartered blooms whose ethereal vapors spur the rose grower to keep forking on the manure.

Give this plant plenty of room. In warmer climes the long stems can be used to arch over walls or adorn trellises. In very cold areas the tips will kill back some, but this rose loves to grow. However, it is not a suckering plant, so it will stay somewhat contained. We never concern ourselves with disease affecting Mme. Plantier. Any spots that may occur on the lustrous, deep green foliage are so few that they are of no consequence.

It is as easy to root as any rose I know.

MORDEN 6910

Hardiness Zone: 3a
Introduced: 1969
Origin: Harp, Canada
Parentage: RSM6119
   × (Pinocchio × (Joanna Hill
   × *Rosa spinosissima altaica*))
Height: 7 ft. (2 m)
Fragrance: f

This is a rose that was never released as a named cultivar yet has found its way into many gardens, and the reason is obvious once you see it in bloom. The large pendulous bush is covered with dark red single flowers with a prominent boss of stamens held aloft by red filaments. Although the plant does not repeat bloom, the show it puts on is spectacular, capable of stopping people in their tracks.

This is a very hardy selection from the Morden Research and Development Centre in Morden, Manitoba, where so many wonderful roses have originated. Apparently this rose was bred by Bert Harp, who preceded Henry Marshall as rose breeder at the station. Harp left no records, nor would he allow any others to see the records of his crosses, so we are not sure how the parentage was discovered. When Marshall arrived at the station this selection was already there.

Morden 6910 is easy to root and produces a vigorous plant in short order.

OSCAR PETERSON

Hardiness Zone: 3b
Introduced: 2016
Origin: Dyck, Canada
Parentage: Yellow Submarine
   × RSMPO2
Height: 7 ft. (2 m)
Fragrance: f

Some call Oscar Peterson the finest jazz pianist of all time. His career spanned 60 years and he garnered five Grammy awards. This rose, from the Canadian Artist Series, honors this Canadian legend.

The plant soars upward, nearly vertically, and is composed of smooth bright green stems. It is an impressively vigorous selection that could make a unique and lovely hedge. It does not appear to sucker. The foliage is impeccably clean, as is the foliage of all the Canadian Artist roses. Best of all, the bush is continuously blooming. This can be enhanced if you take the time to deadhead the finished blossoms, which tend to hang on a bit anyway. Without deadheading you will still have more bloom, but the energy of the plant will be directed toward the formation of the seeds and the deep orange hips that surround them. Deadheading old flowers will stimulate the plant to flower again, so that it can produce still more flowers (and more seeds).

The flower buds are narrow and pointed, flushed with primrose and tipped pink. Although they open to pure sparkling white, in cooler weather the petals are softest yellow and can be subtly blushed with pink tones. The center is a showy, golden-yellow boss of stamens.

This rose is one of the easiest to root of any, and once it rooted grows rapidly.

It has been my experience that white roses are often overlooked and undervalued. Like Oscar's enchanting music, this rose deserves a place of honor — center stage.

POLAREIS

Hardiness Zone: 2b
Introduced: 1988
Origin: Rieksta, Latvia
Parentage: *Rosa rugosa plena*
   Regel × Abelzieds
Height: 8 ft. (2.5 m)
Fragrance: ffff

Nothing stirs the heart of a rose grower quite as much as a new color. When I look at the glistening petals of a Polareis I can't help but think of a strawberry ice that has had most of the syrup sucked out by a child. The subtlety of color in this new rose is its most attractive trait, while its tantalizing fragrance helps to enhance its charm. What is even more striking is the fragrance of the foliage, which I would imagine comes from the cultivar Abelzieds.

This *Rosa rugosa* hybrid has proven very hardy, with foliage that is somewhat textured like its *rugosa* parent but with more gloss. We have seen very little disease on this rose. The bush is well armored with large prickles, and the stems are stiff and angular.

This is an ideal hedging rose. It has size, density and fragrant foliage and flowers, and it does not produce an abundance of suckers. Our stock block of Polareis is a hedge of unparalleled beauty in bloom, which is from June until frost.

It roots readily from cuttings, and we intend to continue propagating this cultivar well into the future.

PRAIRIE PEACE

Hardiness Zone: 2
Introduced: ca. 1975
Origin: Erskine, Canada
Parentage: Beauty of Leafland
   × Hazeldean
Height: 7 ft. (2 m)
Fragrance: ff

Here is a rose bred by a Canadian breeder living at the northern edge of where roses can possibly grow. Though he raised cattle and horses for a living, Robert Erskine found time to use local wild roses and roses bred by fellow breeders living in the colder regions of the Prairies to create a stable of fascinating hardy roses. One of the most enduring is this bicolor rose, named Prairie Peace.

The 20 or so petals of its flower are a soft pink that's shaded yellow toward the central boss of stamens. The bush is fairly vigorous and does not sucker much. The foliage resembles a Scotch rose, no doubt inherited from its pollen parent Hazeldean. Though rarely lasting more than four weeks in bloom, this cultivar is nonetheless much anticipated for its unusual coloration.

Prairie Peace is a unique selection on the list of very hardy roses.

Even those whose skies are often filled with northern lights will find the colors of this rose irresistible.

ROBUSTA

Hardiness Zone: 4a
Introduced: 1987
Origin: Kordes, Germany
Parentage: *Rosa kordesii*
   × *Rosa rugosa*
Height: 8 ft. (2.5 m)
Fragrance: ff

Fallen petals of a Robusta rose have become a meal for a scavenging beetle, but above new crimson flowers unfold. Not all roses have the ability to repeatedly generate new flowers. Many, having performed their yearly fertility rite, pass into the summer's heat clothed only in their greenery. Robusta belongs to that elite and much-prized group of roses that are remontant, or are repeat bloomers.

Although Robusta is simply formed, the size and crimson color ensure that this rose will take a backseat to no others. It is indeed a robust rose. Well-armed stems thrust upward from the plant's base to form a tall, vertical shrub, well suited to frame smaller plants. The combination of very large shiny deep green foliage and wine-red stems is visually exciting. A delicate, fruity fragrance emanates from Robusta, so those who garden for their nose as well as their eyes will not be disappointed.

A 50 percent winter kill back is typical with this rose in our garden, but it inevitably makes a spirited comeback, and by mid-July we are tipping our hats to the skilled hands of Wilhelm Kordes for giving us another healthy and incredibly lovely rose.

It is relatively easy to root, although you will have better success with the lateral shoots that are smaller in diameter.

ROSERAIE DE L'HAY

Hardiness Zone: 3a
Introduced: 1901
Origin: Cochet-Cochet, France
Parentage: *Rosa rugosa*
   rubra o.p.
Height: 10 ft. (3 m)
Fragrance: ffff

Early every summer morning it is my job to pick two or three roses from each cultivar of rose growing in the nursery. They are arranged in bowls on a massive stone table, allowing you to compare the blossoms with ease. This daily exercise is a sacred rite for me. I chart the same course each day and visit the roses in the same order, searching the bushes for the most perfect opening blooms. It is both calming and exhilarating. The last bush I visit is always Roseraie de l'Hay. It reaches well over my head, with dark green foliage and large double blooms that entice the nose with a heavy, sweet perfume.

The dictionary describes the color magenta as deep purplish red. Roseraie de l'Hay is perfect magenta. There are newer Rosa rugosa hybrids that may have more late-season bloom, but few can match the effect of this rose's fascinating petal arrangement. When the high-centered buds open, the outer petals lay flat, the middle petals twist like crepe paper and the innermost petals remain somewhat higher. These flowers appear sterile and do not produce hips.

This easy-to-root rose is absolutely hardy and never shows any sign of disease.

SCABROSA

Hardiness Zone: 2b
Introduced: 1960
Origin: Harkness, UK
Parentage: *Rosa rugosa* seedling
   or hybrid
Height: 10 ft. (3 m)
Fragrance: fff

Although cursed with a most unfortunate name, this wonderful rose is a delight in the garden. Its immense mauve single blooms are its major claim to fame, but I think the most important feature is the bush. Given proper space, this rose will fill a sizable area. It is vigorous and dense with lush, deep green foliage, making it an excellent background plant or a luxuriant hedge. The fragrant and prolific flowers continue throughout the entire season, making the bush a colorful as well as prominent part of the landscape. In fall, the bush becomes a beacon of yellow, red and golden hues. Large, orange-red hips are sprinkled liberally throughout its iridescent foliage, making Scabrosa one of the most attractive roses at the season's end.

This rose becomes more impressive as it ages. When young, Scabrosa is simply another pretty *rugosa* rose. When older, it commands attention with its impressive stature and floral abundance. It is certainly one of the hardiest roses you can grow, and you never need worry about dragging out the sprayer, as it is virtually immune to disease.

It roots well from softwood cuttings taken early in the season, and suckers can be used. Scabrosa is tough, dependable, floriferous and beautiful. It is hard to ask more of a rose.

SCHARLACHGLUT

Hardiness Zone: 4a (possibly 3b)
Introduced: 1952
Origin: Kordes, Germany
Parentage: Poinsettia × Alika
Height: 10 ft. (3 m)
Fragrance: ff

Scharlachglut comes close to the look of crimson velvet. And if ever there were a rose to turn the heads of those who say, "I'm not interested in single roses," this is the one. The English translation of Scharlachglut is "scarlet glow" or "scarlet fire." Neither name can quite capture the intensity of this rose's color.

Part of Scharlachglut's effect lies in its size. It has one of the largest blossoms in our garden, and, in keeping with this grand design, the bush is also large, with thrusting canes that arch slightly. Although a bit open, the bush forms an adequate background for its flowers. Judicious pruning will help to thicken the bush and improve the overall presence of this rose.

We had few hopes for Scharlachglut when it was first planted — fearing it might die in our cold winters — but although it requires some pruning of dead wood each spring, this rose has proven tough. It is generally very healthy and can be rooted from softwood cuttings. It commands a prominent place at our garden's entrance, having convinced us that it intends to stay.

SCOTCH ROSES

Hardiness Zone: 3b
Introduced: Varies
Origin: Varies
Parentage: *Rosa spinosissima* selections and hybrids
Height: up to 7 ft. (2 m) or taller
Fragrance: ffff

The so-called Scotch roses are selections and hybrids of *Rosa spinosissima* (formerly *Rosa pimpinellifolia*). These were native to Europe and in the United Kingdom were very popular in the 19th century. They vary in height, but most will grow to 7 ft. (2 m) or taller. A few are more diminutive. We have included a selection on the opposite page to show the variety this group contains.

In Europe and North America a number of breeders used this species to provide hardiness to their hybrids. A few include Aïcha, Karl Förster, Prairie Peace, Harison's Yellow and Stanwell Perpetual.

The typical foliage is composed of small leaflets. The stems tend to be thin and wiry, although some hybrids have thicker stems. Virtually all selections and most hybrids have the powerful fragrance typical of the species.

Growers should be warned that many of these plants are aggressive growers and may occupy a good deal of space. They can grow impenetrably dense, and pruning them is a challenge for the most game of gardeners. Most will sucker extensively, though some hybrids do not. This makes them ideal for where a vast expanse of roses is required or where a bank needs stabilization.

Most root readily, but some hybrids may be a bit more finicky.

This pure white Scotch rose selection exhibits the characteristic fragrance of the species.

The name of this light pink Scotch rose has been lost.

Rosa spinosissima altaica is a selection of the species that exhibits the density of the bush.

◀ This unusual hybrid called Doorenbos is a low plant with rich magenta blooms.

SNOW PAVEMENT

Hardiness Zone: 2b
Introduced: 1986
Origin: Baum, Germany
Parentage: unknown, *Rosa rugosa* hybrid
Height: 7 ft. (2 m)
Fragrance: ffff

The color of Snow Pavement, also known by its original name Schneeköppe, is white, delicately suffused with lavender — the color of a violet sunset reflected off snow. This rare pastel is a welcome addition to any garden.

At a distance the blooms appear white; it is only when you come closer that the soft coloring becomes apparent. What draws us deeper into the blossoms is a rich, heady fragrance and unusually long buds that resemble fat, stubby cigars. These expand into very large flowers.

The bush is dense and vigorous. It spreads rapidly outward, making it an excellent choice for covering banks or other large areas. Its density also makes it a wonderful choice for a hedge. The foliage is a paragon of health — I know of no healthier leaves in the rose world. Its only foe is an order of insects, thrips, which distort the outside petals. Once their time is done, though, most blooms are perfect. The rose is very easy to root.

The choice of Snow Pavement as an English name is unfortunate, as the bush is not a flat ground cover as the name suggests, and the plant is distinctly more pleasant than asphalt. However, a name is just that. The rose is real, and any name would never do it justice.

SOUVENIR DE PHILEMON COCHET

Hardiness Zone: 2b
Introduced: 1899
Origin: Cochet, France
Parentage: sport of Blanc Double de Coubert
Height: 7 ft. (2 m)
Fragrance: ffff

Occasionally a rose will throw what is called a "sport." Something causes a change in the morphology within the bud where the sport initiates. From that point on that section of the plant will be different. Sports might include those that change the color of the flower, increase the production of flowers and/or fruits, or produce an increased number of flower petals. If someone discovers such a sport and propagates it, they have a new cultivar. However, sports can be unstable and may revert back to the original growth pattern.

Souvenir de Philemon Cochet is a stable sport of the well-known pure white rose Blanc Double de Coubert. In every respect but one, it is identical to the rose from which it sprang. It contains more than double the number of petals than there are in the original Blanc. It is as if a Blanc Double de Coubert flower opens to reveal an extra flower whose petals twist and swirl in its center. In cool weather there will be a touch of pink, but once open it is a pure white.

Souvenir is very hardy, vigorous and clothed in lustrous, deep green leaves, and it flowers in waves through the season. Best of all, it has the same rich, heady fragrance of its mother. Softwood cuttings root relatively easily if taken early in the season just as flowering commences, and suckers can be used.

Give this plant lots of room and it will fill it. Although not as prone to suckering as some, it will continue to grow outward until it occupies a sizable piece of real estate. And be forewarned — a long period of rain during blooming can leave the flowers soggy and brown. The balance to this is when sunny days reign, this rose is a souvenir that will always be treasured.

WASAGAMING

Hardiness Zone: 2b
Introduced: 1939
Origin: Skinner, Canada
Parentage: (*Rosa rugosa* × *Rosa aicularis*) × Gruss an Teplitz
Height: 10 ft. (3 m)
Fragrance: fff

For those to whom size matters, meet the rose that challenges all comers. Without preventative pruning this plant will top 10 ft. (3 m) or more. Its stems can be as thick as tree branches. Yet the attentive gardener can keep this beast in bounds with a pair of shears and loppers. This is a great rose for the back of a large bed or where a behemoth would be welcome.

The blooms are large as well and quite double, but it is the color that attracts attention. The flower is lavender-rose and built in much the same way as a peony flower. When this bush is in full bloom it is staggering to behold. Even after the initial flush the rose will keep flowering until frost.

This uncommon rose was created by Dr. Frank Leith Skinner, a skilled breeder of many species who worked in Dropmore, Manitoba — a place where winter temperatures routinely drop to –40°F (–40°C). In order to create plants that could tolerate such extreme cold, he imported seeds of species from far-flung northern areas such as Siberia.

He communicated with breeders around the world, and his work has been hailed by many.

To create Wasagaming, he used *Rosa rugosa*, which he crossed with a native rose in his area called *Rosa aicularis*. He obtained a promising seedling that was then crossed with a famous Bourbon rose named Gruss an Teplitz, a fragrant, double, red repeat bloomer. Wasagaming was the payoff for his accumulated knowledge and steady patience. It was certainly worth the effort.

This rose roots readily and will grow strongly afterward.

WILLIAM LOBB

Hardiness Zone: 4a
Introduced: 1855
Origin: Laffay, France
Parentage: unknown, *Rosa centifolia muscosa* hybrid
Height: 7 ft. (2 m)
Fragrance: fff

People are slowly awakening to the immense body of plants that have been neglected and deserve more important places in the garden. Perhaps with this exciting trend gaining momentum, we will soon see such cultivars as William Lobb in more gardens.

William Lobb is the English name of a French rose, Duchesse d'Istrie. To further confuse matters, its sensuous purple-crimson blooms inspired the name Old Velvet Moss. Whatever name you prefer, this rose is a welcome addition to the northern garden. Its extreme vigor is matched by its tremendous hardiness.

In our garden the long, prickly stems are rarely touched by even the coldest winters, and after a few years of extraordinary growth, the bush becomes an imposing part of any rose bed. For this reason, be sure to give the plant room. As well, you may want to give it some support. Its long stems are somewhat lax, and the numerous blossoms, which come in large clusters, weigh the stems down.

This is one of the Moss roses, a group of roses whose buds and upper stems are covered by tiny prickles that are soft and resemble moss. William Lobb has a great abundance of these peculiar aberrations. The flower itself is very double and well formed with a delightful fragrance. Although the blooms are only medium in size, the sheer number of them will create a dazzling display.

William Lobb is also fairly easy to root from softwood cuttings.

8

SEMIVIGOROUS SHRUBS

Shrubs growing up to 7 ft. (2 m)

◀ Frü Dagmar Hastrup is a selection of *Rosa rugosa* that is often touted as low growing, but it can grow far taller than you might expect.

AGNES

Hardiness Zone: 3a
Introduced: 1922
Origin: Saunders, Canada
Parentage: *Rosa rugosa × Rosa foetida persiana*
Height: 5 ft. (1.5 m)
Fragrance: fff

Agnes was the first named cultivar produced by Canadian breeder Dr. William Saunders, who was the head of the Dominion Research Station in Ottawa. Sometime in the late 1800s he bred this rose using *Rosa rugosa* and Persian Yellow, a double form of *Rosa foetida*. The result was an amber-yellow double rose that is subtly suffused with apricot when opening and subtle pink tones in cool weather. As the flower ages it turns toward ivory.

It is interesting that, while *Rosa rugosa* has been used extensively to try and produce hardy yellow roses, the successes have been few and far between. This is one of the earliest and most enchanting results.

This rose has many attributes that recommend it as deserving a favored place in your garden. The delightful fruity fragrance of this rose is as essential a part of its character as is its pastel petals. These flowers adorn a bush that is exceptionally hardy, and the crinkled lime green leaves are seldom if ever bothered by disease.

The bad news is that Agnes is difficult to find. You are more likely to find it growing in Europe than North America. It is nearly always budded or grafted, but suckers can be used if you can find a robust plant on its own roots. Success with cuttings has eluded many propagators. We have only rooted a few. However, if you have a masochistic bent, you can give it a try. The cuttings should be taken just before flowering. Avoid over misting. A carefully controlled humidity tent or low cold frame may encourage some success.

For many this rose is a bit fragile. Its petals are delicate and will not stand up to heavy wind and rain. This lack of substance can be called a fault, but the loose, carefree blooms of Agnes have an undeniable charm that stiff, more formal flowers can never achieve — a crown for fairies rather than kings.

ALAIN BLANCHARD

Hardiness Zone: 4a (possibly 3b)
Introduced: 1839
Origin: Vibert, France
Parentage: *Rosa centifolia* × *Rosa gallica* hybrid
Height: 4 ft. (1.25 m)
Fragrance: fff

There are a great number of *Rosa gallica* hybrids that deserve a place in the northern garden, and it is difficult to choose those that stand out as exceptional because so many are fascinating. Some have immense blooms, others an inordinate number of petals.

Alain Blanchard is neither a giant nor very double. What it

has is unique coloration: the red petals are spotted with darker red patches. Instead of looking sickly or weird, the combination is both appealing and riveting. It would be interesting to know if this coloring was on the original plant or if its genes have mutated. Like most *gallicas*, the blossoms are quite fragrant. Alain Blanchard is also a hardy bush that is easy to grow and does not get overly large. It will spread with time if allowed. The leaves are deepest green and heavily textured. This is a very special rose for a collector.

Alain Blanchard roots fairly easily.

CAREFREE BEAUTY

Hardiness: Zone 3b
Introduced: before 1976
Origin: Buck, USA
Parentage: (Applejack × ((Dean Collins × Queen Elizabeth) × (Independence × Improved Lafayette))) × Prairie Princess
Height: 4 ft. (1.25 m)
Fragrance: fff

Griffith Buck has never received the accolades he deserves for his breeding work. Working at the University of Iowa, he produced a large number of excellent hardy roses. Unfortunately, many are difficult to find or nearly obsolete. But one that is still widely grown and available is Carefree Beauty.

The bush is an upright to lax plant with relatively thin stems

and medium green glossy foliage that is among the most disease resistant I know. The flowers are medium pink, fading to soft pink. The opening buds are exquisitely formed, similar to that of the grandiflora rose Queen Elizabeth, one of its parents. The semidouble blooms open to very large flowers that have a fragrance that is delicately sweet but never cloying.

We have grown this rose for nearly 30 years, and in all that time it has never failed us. Hardiness, health, form, charm and fragrance all in one plant. If you can find sources, try some of Buck's other selections, including Applejack, Hawkeye Belle, Honey Sweet, Distant Drums, Prairie Princess and many others. Hopefully, more people will propagate

the many introductions he gave the world.

Carefree Beauty is easy to root.

CHARLES ALBANEL

Charles Albanel is virtually unknown in the gardening scene. Its parent is Souvenir de Philemon Cochet, the very double sport of Blanc Double de Coubert. It has the hardiness of its parent as well as a similar bush form, though slightly more compact. It was introduced as a low-growing plant,

but we have found it to be quite vigorous. In time it will form a wide plant that will blanket an embankment or garden bed with its dense foliage and informal blooms. The new stems are medium green and turn blackish with age, and the branches are well-armed with prickles. The rose hips are medium-sized, orange-red and a flattened globular shape.

The semi-double flowers are a pleasing pinkish mauve. They begin in late spring and continue until the very end of the season. Compared to similar cultivars, we've found Charles Albanel has the very best of fall displays.

Both the hardiness and disease

Hardiness Zone: 2b
Introduced: 1982
Origin: Svejda, Canada
Parentage: Souvenir de Philemon Cochet o.p.
Height: 5 ft. (1.5 m)
Fragrance: fff

resistance of this rose are exceptional. It is virtually immune to mildew and blackspot. Given all these attributes, I have no doubt that this cultivar will become increasingly common in the garden and in public and commercial plantings. To propagate, take cuttings early in the season just as flowering starts.

CHINOOK SUNRISE

Hardiness Zone: 3b
Introduced: 2019
Origin: Conev and Sandhu, Canada
Parentage: 20ALFR05 (Astrid Lindgren × Frontenac) × 27SPO412 (Yellow Submarine × PO4 (Scarlet Meidiland × Frontenac))
Height: 4 ft. (1.25 m) or more
Fragrance: f

as soft vermilion buds, then shifting to tones of coral and salmon. This unusual coloration was key to its being chosen as one of the roses of the 49th Parallel Series from the Vineland Research and Innovation Centre in Ontario. These roses go through rigorous testing procedures to insure they are highly disease resistant, continuously blooming and hardy across much of Canada. Apart from these imperatives, the rose should have a color that appeals to the public. To this end Vineland polled the public to see what colors they most desired in flowers. From this came Chinook Sunrise's unique coral hue — a color favored by many. And you would be hard-pressed to find a person who does not admire the

splendor of this sunrise.

The bush is moderately vigorous and will grow well in Zone 4. It is definitely worth trying to grow in Zone 3b. The plant is very resistant to blackspot and mildew. It does have some sensitivity to *Cercospora rosicola*, commonly called frog eye, but this has little effect on the appearance of a well-grown plant. It also roots very easily from softwood cuttings taken as the flower buds form.

The name of a rose can be all important in deciding how popular it becomes. While names often have nothing to do with the qualities of a rose, they can elicit a response in the buyer that stimulates impulse buying. In the case of Chinook Sunrise, the name fits.

Like a sunrise, the colors of this rose change as it unfolds, starting

CINNAMON

Hardiness Zone: 3a
Introduced: unknown, probably before 1583
Origin: unknown, Europe
Parentage: possibly a double form of *Rosa cinnamomea*, but this is disputed
Height: 4 ft. (1.25 m) or more
Fragrance: fff

My home in New Brunswick is in a rural area. Scattered throughout the region are old cellar holes enclosed by crumbling stone walls that once supported the now vanished houses — walls built of stones cleared by the farmers from their fields as far back as the 19th century. The verges and bottoms of these depressions are now home to wild raspberry, apple and spruce, but what often catches my eye in summer are thickets of Cinnamon roses, the survivors of bushes planted perhaps 100 years ago or more. This is an extraordinary testament to the tenacity and hardiness of these plants. These thickets are dense with wiry stems that repel anyone foolish enough to pit themselves against this bulwark of briars. Even where trees have overtaken the sky above them, the roses seem to persist. Most Cinnamon roses in full sun only grow to 4 ft. (1.25 m) tall, but these plants have been grown far taller.

No doubt passed from farm to farm as suckers dug from existing bushes, Cinnamon would have been a symbol of permanence and of being home, as well as a beautiful thing to brighten lives that were often hard. Most roses would not have lasted long without rigorous attention, but once planted this rose would stand unbowed by the insults of weather and lack of care.

It is plain to see why this rose was so beloved then. Besides toughness, there is the flower, a dense mass of frilled pink petals with intense fragrance, more clove than cinnamon. One would be pardoned for musing that some mad scientist had made an impossible cross between a rose and a carnation. Like the carnation, the small flowers are borne in clusters that begin flowering later than most roses and continue for four weeks.

If you are going to propagate this rose it is important that you take cuttings just as flowering begins. If taken too late, your percentage of successful rooting will wane.

The origins of this rose have not yet been unraveled. Though often referred to as a cultivar of *Rosa cinnamomea*, this is only surmise. Some claim it was discovered in North America, but most rose historians believe it was found in Europe as early as the 16th century. It probably arrived in Quebec by boat from France and spread from there. Perhaps someday when the DNA sleuths are not as busy, they will be able to sort out the mystery — but then again, what's wrong with a bit of mystery?

DART'S DASH

This *rugosa* hybrid is our go-to rose when someone asks for a good hedging rose. It is dense and forms a good-sized symmetrical bush. While very similar to the older Hansa rose, Dart's Dash has better flower form, a larger bloom, a longer blooming season and larger hips. In fact, the hips of this rose are among the largest. More importantly, they have a thicker outer covering of flesh than any we have tried (and we have nibbled on many). The hips are best just after a frost, when the flesh has somewhat softened. If you're a maker of rose hip jam you should definitely seek out this cultivar. And you can still enjoy the fragrance of the late blooms

Hardiness Zone: 2b
Introduced: ca. 1980
Origin: Darthuis Nursery, Netherlands
Parentage: unknown, *Rosa rugosa* hybrid
Height: 6 ft. (1.75 m)
Fragrance: fff

while having your snack, as Dart's Dash will bloom until hard frost.

The bush is virtually immune to blackspot, though you may see a touch of mildew late in the season, but it is not serious enough to weaken the bush. Dart's Dash also roots very easily. All in all, this is one of the best of the mauve *rugosas*.

DELICATA

This is an underappreciated early *Rosa rugosa* hybrid that should be much better known. When Cooling was creating Delicata, *Rosa rugosa* had only been recently introduced into Europe from Japan, and only a few grew it. Using it for hybridization was a forward-thinking idea.

Though its double flowers may have appeared delicate to its originator, Delicata is definitely not a delicate plant. In many ways it is a typical *rugosa* shrub, being dense, spreading and growing tall, if allowed. Its foliage is very healthy and a medium green. The flowers, however, are among the few that are close to a true pink — most others being what I call mauve-pink. I think the only other comparable *rugosa* hybrid is Sarah Van Fleet, but Delicata is far hardier.

If there is a fault, it is that the rose will quickly spread sideways by suckering. This limits its use to gardens that can benefit from

Hardiness Zone: 3a
Introduced: 1898
Origin: Cooling, UK
Parentage: unknown, *Rosa rugosa* hybrid
Height: 5 ft. (1.5 m)
Fragrance: fff

a large imposing plant. On the other hand, any rose can be kept in its place by regular pruning and removal of unwanted suckers. We prune this rose back every two years or so and have kept it in a 7 ft. by 7 ft. (2 m by 2 m) space for nearly 20 years.

Delicata is easy to root from cuttings if taken early in the season. It is also easy to find suckers to use for propagation.

DR. MERKELEY

Hardiness Zone: 2b
Introduction: 1924 (by Frank Leith Skinner)
Origin: unknown, believed to be northern Russia
Parentage: unknown
Height: 6 ft. (1.75 m)
Fragrance: fff

At the end of World War I a Canadian soldier returned home from his duty in Siberia with a most unusual souvenir. It was a very double pink rose with a heavenly scent, and this rose came with roots attached. According to a letter I received from the son of Dr. H.J. Merkeley — a dentist who practiced in Winnipeg, Manitoba, in the 1920s — his father took a piece of this rose, presumably from the soldier's original plant, as payment for services rendered. Dr. Merkeley knew the breeder Frank Leith Skinner, who also owned Skinner Nursery, at that time a struggling young nursery in Dropmore, Manitoba. Skinner immediately saw the value of this ultra-hardy rose and began growing it. He introduced it to the world in 1924 as Dr. Merkeley, a dedication to the man who had gifted him the cutting.

Here was a rose that could survive the coldest of sites and still produce elegantly cupped flowers with a form reminiscent of a Damask or *alba* rose. It also makes me think of the old cultivar Rose de Meaux. Unless DNA analysis is done on Dr. Merkeley, we may never know the exact origin and makeup of this unusual rose.

The very center is a button surrounded by perhaps 20 pillowy petals. Multitudes of larger petals swirl around the depressed middle, giving the flower the effect of a whirlpool of pink petals. It is late coming into bloom, flowering in profusion when most other roses are resting from their first flush.

Rooting it is relatively easy. With proper conditions at least three-quarters of the cuttings will form good plants.

FANTIN-LATOUR

Hardiness Zone: 4a
Introduced: 1945
Origin: Bunyard, UK
Parentage: unknown, *Rosa centifolia* hybrid
Height: 4 ft. (1.25 m)
Fragrance: ffff

I can only imagine the excitement that Edward Bunyard experienced when he discovered this rose. We will likely never know where the rose was originally bred or what its exact parentage is, but it really does not make a difference. The important thing is that it is here in the present, saved from extinction.

This rose is named after the French painter Henri Fantin-Latour, who was well-known for his romantic depictions of roses. This rose is certainly well named, for it typifies the romantic image of what a rose should be. The soft pink double flower darkens somewhat toward the middle. The many petals often arrange themselves into four quadrants — a form that is both contained and informal at the same time.

If fragrance is your game, you should make it your quest to find this rose. It has a deep and sensuous aroma that should tantalize even the most jaded of sniffers. The plant grows upward and, in warmer climes, can be used as a low climber. In Zone 4 it will kill back some, but it is hardy enough to maintain enough old wood to have a good show.

The deep green foliage is quite healthy. Though supposedly prone to mildew, this grower has never seen it attack the leaves. You might see a bit of blackspot on older leaves, but not enough to give you a problem.

If cuttings are taken early in the flowering season, they will root well.

FRONTENAC

Hardiness: Zone 3b
Introduced: 1993
Origin: Svejda, Canada
Parentage: (Queen Elizabeth × (Double Red Simonet × Von Scharnhorst)) × Felix Leclerc
Height: 5 ft. (1.5 m)
Fragrance: ff

Charming deep fuchsia-pink blossoms adorn the stems of Frontenac. The foliage is glossy and just a shade lighter than spruce green. You will not see mildew or blackspot on this plant, and the semidouble blooms will continue until frost.

These are wonderful attributes for a northern rose, and there is a

bit of a story to this plant. Felicitas Svejda, the breeder of the Explorer Series (and later the Canadian Artist Series) relied extensively on Frontenac to produce seedlings with similar attributes. Many of the Explorer Series roses have Frontenac in their bloodlines.

The bush has presence, but does not outgrow its welcome. After 30 years in our garden it has not suckered. Though not as commonly found as some of the other Explorer roses, if you see one give it a place. The warmth of its blooms will repay the cost in coin.

FRÜ DAGMAR HASTRUP

Hardiness Zone: 2b (possibly 2a)
Introduced: 1914
Origin: Hastrup, Denmark
Parentage: unknown, *Rosa rugosa* seedling
Height: 6 ft. (1.75 m)
Fragrance: fff

If there were such a thing as pink spiders that wove cloth, their silken product might resemble the petals of Frü Dagmar Hastrup. The light pink flowers shimmer in the light. They are large and, when opening, resemble chalices. Best of all, they do not stop blooming until freezing temperatures put an end to their prolific beauty. The flowers are also pleasingly fragrant.

This super hardy rose is fairly compact, becoming more wide than tall, but it is not a low grower, as many would have us believe. Hedges in my garden grow nearly 7 ft. (2 m) high. Frü Dagmar Hastrup is very well protected — the prickles are so numerous that there is no smooth stem surface. Its formidable armor is made up of both short and somewhat longer prickles. The plant is very healthy, being nearly immune to blackspot and mildew. Hips are numerous and large, useful for those growers who enjoy these vitamin-packed fruits.

One of the most endearing qualities of Frü Dagmar Hastrup is its fall foliage. As the daylight hours wane, the green leaves take on a deep maroon tone. The process continues until the foliage changes to deep golden-yellow with coppery highlights that seem iridescent. Although I have

always enjoyed this rose's blooms in summer, I will never forget the first time I stood transfixed in my garden as the late afternoon sun glanced off the glowing autumn leaves of this gem. I still have not found a rose with a more exciting transition into winter.

Frü Dagmar Hastrup is fairly easy to root from cuttings, and suckers can be used. It will be small at first, but will gain vigor as it goes into its second season.

GEORGE VANCOUVER

Hardiness Zone: 3b
Introduced: 1994
Origin: Svejda, Canada
Parentage: L83 (*Rosa kordesii* × G49) × E10 (seedling of complex origin)
Height: 4 ft. (1.25 m)
Fragrance: f

The Canadian Explorer Series of roses has given the northern rose grower some of the most reliable varieties now available. One of the later selections is George Vancouver. This superb introduction is one of the hardiest of the non-rugosa types. Plants that have endured −30°F (−35°C) show little or no damage. It is also a plant with a neat habit and deep green, shiny foliage. It is not overly vigorous, instead forming a wide, rounded bush with deep red stems.

The flowers start in early summer, and in fall the bush is still laden with blooms. Blossoms are borne in clusters. Each semidouble bloom is a neat arrangement of scalloped petals, symmetrical but not stiff. The color of the flowers is a subtle blend of red and orange as the buds open, giving a subdued scarlet look, fading to dark pink before falling cleanly off the bush. This is a rose that will win your admiration and affection over the years. It is also a very easy rose to root.

HANSALAND

Hardiness Zone: 4a (possibly 3b)
Introduced: 1993
Origin: Kordes, Germany
Parentage: unknown, *Rosa rugosa* hybrid
Height: 4 ft. (1.25 m)
Fragrance: f

The world of hardy roses would be much diminished without the work of the Kordes family of Germany. Hansaland is yet another example of an introduction that is tough, healthy and strikingly attractive. This rose should not be confused with Hansa, a much older *Rosa rugosa* selection that is a double mauve-red bloom.

The semidouble flowers of Hansaland are large and informal with true-red petals that seem to shout at you from a distance. Beware, however, of the stems. They are well armed and not to be messed with unless you are protected by adequate leather gloves. The foliage shows a mix of traits from the two different parents — in this case the textural influence of the *Rosa rugosa* parent and the shiny surface inherited from its other mysteriously withheld parent.

We do see some blackspot, particularly in late summer, but this does not affect the plant's overall appearance. In Zone 4 you may have a bit of tip damage in a harsh winter, but we find that a light pruning each spring is actually advantageous, keeping the bush denser. You needn't worry about losing blooms, as this rose flowers on new wood as well as old and will give you color from late spring to frost.

Be sure to harvest cuttings before the flower buds open, and you should have good luck rooting them.

HENRI MARTIN

Hardiness Zone: 4a
Introduced: 1863
Origin: Laffay, France
Parentage: unknown, *Rosa centifolia muscosa*
Height: 4 ft. (1.25 m)
Fragrance: fff

The Moss roses are a most unusual group. They had their beginnings in the 17th century, when one of the *Rosa centifolia* roses, often referred to as Cabbage roses, underwent a strange mutation. Small, soft prickles that resembled moss appeared along the stems and on the bases of the flowers. This freakish rose was cultivated and eventually bred to create several cultivars of Moss roses with a wide range of flower colors. Although a number of these are quite hardy and well adapted to northern gardens, Henri Martin has a special place in my garden because of its masses of crimson red flowers.

In early summer Henri Martin is a fountain of blossoms. Each cluster is carried by rather slender, wiry stems with prickles that are deceptively harmless-looking, as well as the rather soft prickles. The bush is generally upright, but somewhat lax and spreading.

Although winter injury necessitates pruning some of the bush back, most of the bush survives, and its ability to spring back is remarkable. Henri Martin is fairly easy to root if the cuttings are taken early. The deep orange hips, which appear in the fall, are small and vase-shaped.

Moss roses add a distinctive and curious bit of variety to the palette of common roses, and isn't variety the spice that compels most of us to seek yet more plants to fill our overflowing garden beds?

HENRY HUDSON

I have a rare, single red peony in my garden. With its ferny foliage, this peony is very beautiful when it's in bloom, but what makes it stand out is the background of snow-white Henry Hudson roses that form a backdrop to the plant. This prolifically blooming rose is another valuable introduction from Agriculture Canada's Explorer Series.

Henry Hudson has virtually everything you could ask for. Its deep green and copious foliage is free of disease, it is absolutely hardy, its flowers bloom continuously in waves, it is richly fragrant and its pink-tipped buds open to a sparkling show of white petals.

This important addition to the list of hardy roses is like an explorer of the north — it can be found surviving in the coldest of places.

Although originally touted as a very low-growing plant, we have found Henry can grow quite tall. It has great density, which makes it ideal as a hedge. Its spreading nature is perfect for covering banks or as a massing plant in parks or along road medians.

Be forewarned — like most *Rosa rugosas*, Henry Hudson is well armored with sharp prickles. It also holds on to its spent blooms, so you may want to pick the old flowers for best appearance. But if you don't you

Hardiness Zone: 2b
Introduced: 1979
Origin: Svejda, Canada
Parentage: *Rosa rugosa* Schneezwerg o.p.
Height: 5 ft. (1.5 m)
Fragrance: fff

will have a lovely crop of small orange-red hips in the fall.

Propagating Henry Hudson from softwood cuttings gives variable results. The best results are with cuttings from early season growth, just at early flowering. New plants will be small, but time will solve any vigor handicap. Suckers can be used as well.

J.P. CONNELL

Hardiness Zone: 4a
Introduced: 1987
Origin: Svejda, Canada
Parentage: Arthur Bell
   × Von Scharnhorst o.p.
Height: 5 ft. (1.5 m)
Fragrance: fff

This rose has become associated with the Canadian Explorer Series. It was released during the same period the Explorers were being released, but it is derived from a completely different breeding line and is not related to the others in the series. It was named to honor a retiring director of the Ottawa Research Station.

Whatever the circumstances, this rose is deserving of recognition. It has an elegant form, and its petals are a rich, warm yellow that fade to cream. When well sited it can grow to impressive heights, highlighting its extreme verticality.

Although somewhat prone to blackspot, the disease that haunts nearly all yellow roses, J.P. Connell fills an important niche in the inventory of hardy roses. Waves of symmetrical, fully double and high-centered blooms appear throughout the season. If anything, the later flowers seem larger and more impressive, and they make lovely cut flowers. The plentiful foliage is a rich green, and it grows on stiff yellow-green stems that hold the elegant blooms skyward.

With a little extra attention, this valuable introduction can transform a piece of your garden into an exciting showcase for one of the hardier yellow roses. Layering or budding may be the best way to propagate J.P. Connell, which is moderately difficult to root.

KAKWA

Hardiness Zone: 2a
Introduced: 1973
Origin: Wallace, Canada
Parentage: unknown, *Rosa spinosissima* hybrid
Height: 4 ft. (1.25 m)
Fragrance: ffff

As the late spring nights lose that cool edge, and the early spring flowers are reduced to simple greenery, the rose grower's anticipation heightens. The sight of those first unfolding buds is exhilarating and rejuvenating. In our garden it is Kakwa that first appears. Almost overnight, this reliable and carefree rose becomes blanketed so thickly with blossoms that the foliage is virtually hidden under their delicate weight. This petaled coverlet is creamy white from a distance, but as you approach, the subtle pink tones of these double blooms become apparent. Another wonderful aspect of this early rose is its intense fragrance. I recommend you keep your nose at a slight distance from the flowers. Putting your nose into a Kakwa blossom is a bit like sticking it into a bottle of perfume.

The bush is an extremely adaptable one. It will grow in fairly poor soils and prefers a lighter, well-drained soil. Like most of the Scotch roses, you will need to keep an eye on this plant as it ages. It is a wanderer and will try to claim more territory if allowed. Keep it thinned as well. Untended plants will become so dense they are difficult to deal with. This is a remarkably tough and hardy plant, it is easy to root if cuttings

are taken early and it will grow for almost any northern gardener.

Although few roses have such an effect in bloom, Kakwa soon gives way to the many roses vying for our attentions. It is as if it gives everything it has in one exuberant burst of energy and then collapses to await the raising of the next spring curtain. Some may call it a bit part, but it acts its role with such energy that I would hate to think of the play without it.

KARL FÖRSTER

Hardiness Zone: 4a
Introduced: 1953
Origin: Kordes, Germany
Parentage: Frau Karl Drushki
  × *Rosa spinosissima altaica*
Height: 5 ft. (1.5 m)
Fragrance: fff

Some roses have a way of tapping you on the shoulder and saying, "Take a look at me." My first Karl Förster plants sat at the edge of the garden for two years without attracting much attention. Then, in their third spring, they erupted with a display that took us by surprise. Shapely pointed buds by the hundreds unfolded into loose blossoms the color of whipped cream, until the foliage virtually disappeared under this unique topping.

Karl Förster would not let us forget this extravaganza. As a reminder, it continued to bloom throughout the summer and early fall, an amazing feat for a Scotch rose hybrid. An added feature of this prolific bloomer is the red color of the new stems. Contrasted against the gray-green leaves, they create a characteristic look to this rose.

All these wonderful attributes mean nothing to us if the rose does not perform well in our merciless winters. Karl Förster has passed the test with exceptional honors. It seems to have inherited the toughness of its Scotch rose parent as well as the flowering ability of its hybrid tea parent — a near perfect combination. If there is any fault it is that it will ball in wet weather.

Karl Förster is often budded or grafted. It can be rooted from softwood cuttings, but the cuttings require careful attention just after rooting or they can drop their leaves and die.

LINDA CAMPBELL

Hardiness Zone: 4a (possibly 3b)
Introduced: 1991
Origin: Moore, USA
Parentage: Anytime × *Rosa rugosa* Magnifica
Height: 5 ft. (1.5 m)
Fragrance: ff

Ralph Moore is one of the most dynamic rose breeders the world has known. He has created fascinating color combinations, oak-shaped leaves and many other wonders. His use of *Rosa rugosa* for some of his crosses has given the hardy rose grower real gems, like Linda Campbell.

The bush pushes upward and then arches outward. The stems have a texture faintly reminiscent of velvety deer antlers, only in hues of red and green. The flowers are deep red with a touch of white highlighting the bases of the center petals. The double flowers are borne on clusters so large that a single stem in hand is a bouquet. Keep this plant well fed and happy, and it will create a red temple of color.

Temperatures colder than –22°F (–30°C) will cause some winter damage to stem tips, but even when pruned back by arctic highs, they rebound and will rebloom quickly after their first flush in early summer. Resistance to blackspot is fair, but lower leaves will be affected when conditions favor this disease. Happily, mildews and rusts are not problems. This is an easy rose to root.

MARIE BUGNET

Hardiness Zone: 2b
Introduced: 1963
Origin: Bugnet, Canada
Parentage: (Thérèse Bugnet × unnamed seedling) × F.J. Grootendorst
Height: 3 ft. (1 m)
Fragrance: fff

This rose is slowly rising from obscurity to claim its long overdue recognition. Its relative, Thérèse Bugnet, is known throughout the rose world, but Marie has remained unknown, except to a few collectors of heritage roses. It is not a tall plant but does spread rapidly by suckering, making it unwelcome in a tidy bed but a perfect rose for a bank or low hedge. Its *Rosa rugosa* heritage is clearly visible in its textured leaves, which rarely show any disease. The double blooms are preceded by buds of white that are streaked deep pink. They open purest white and very shapely and they continue to appear until frost.

If there is a fault in this rose it is the delicacy of the petals. In wet weather the outer petals can become saturated with water and brown, not allowing the bud to open fully. However, this fault should not discourage the northern gardener from planting Marie, for though its flowers are delicate, the bush is tenacious and will survive temperatures of –40°F (–40°C) with ease. And the form — as the buds start to unfurl an arrangement of petals appears that will hold your attention every time.

One other thing to watch for is the gall wasp. This tiny insect seems to relish the wood of this rose. Be vigilant and you can nip this problem in the stem as soon as it is noticed.

Marie Bugnet also roots easily.

MARIE-VICTORIN

Hardiness Zone: 4a (possibly 3b)
Introduced: 1998
Origin: Svejda, Canada
Parentage: (Queen Elizabeth
   × Arthur Bell) × L83
Height: 4 ft. (1.25 m)
Fragrance: fff

It fascinates me that the colors we see in a rose are not those absorbed by the petals, but rather they are the spectrum of light that is reflected off the petals — the discards, as it were. Each rose reflects a unique blend of colors, and one of the most unusual reflections bounces off the blossoms of Marie-Victorin. The petals of this Canadian Explorer Series rose reflect silvery-pink, with edges and undersides of soft yellow. The combination is enchanting.

The scent released by this flower is a perfect balance between sweetness and lightness — a most wonderful addiction. This is also an exquisitely structured flower. The buds are pointed and unfurl into a symmetrical double bloom. The bush is moderately vigorous and hardy enough to grow well in Zone 4, with only slight winter kill. In more humid years blackspot can appear on the older foliage. A series of preventative sulfur sprays in early spring and summer can prevent this.

This rose is named after Brother Marie-Victorin Kirouac, the man who founded the Montreal Botanical Garden, a treasure house of plants from around the world and the home of a wonderful rose collection.

MME. HARDY

Hardiness Zone: 4a
Introduced: 1831
Origin: Hardy, France
Parentage: unknown, *Rosa
   centifolia/Rosa damascena*
Height: 5 ft. (1.5 m)
Fragrance: ffff

Although often classified as an *alba* rose, Mme. Hardy would be more correctly labeled a Damask rose. It is a classic white with copious petals that arrange themselves into a perfectly symmetrical quartered form. The color is the purest of whites, and in the center lies a bright green pip.

The sight of this rose in bloom draws me back constantly, and I often pick one to float in a glass bowl, its perfection of form and color needing no further decoration. Oh, and the fragrance. The Damask genes in Mme. Hardy harken back to Persian gardens, where the Damask rose once beckoned sultans and lucky plebeians to inhale its sweet aromas.

The bush is stiff and upright with foliage that ranks among the most disease resistant of any old garden rose. The plant is also relatively easy to root.

There are few roses that command such loyalty to their charms. Mme. Hardy is one that has legions of adoring adherents.

MOJE HAMMARBERG

Hardiness Zone: 3b
Introduced: 1931
Origin: Hammarberg, Sweden
Parentage: unknown, *Rosa rugosa* hybrid
Height: 5 ft. (1.5 m)
Fragrance: fff

There are many double mauve-red *rugosa* roses. To accurately identify cultivars that are so similar, it is necessary to examine the details of petal shape, form and edge. Do the petals bleed into other colors near their base? What is the shape of the sepals that encase the petals until they fold back as the flower opens? What is the exact shape of the leaf and the pattern of the serrated edge? These are the vernal equivalent to fingerprints that point you toward the correct identification.

In order for a rose propagator to ensure the roses they produce are properly named, it is necessary to maintain a known specimen of each cultivar. It might require one, or two, or a dozen or a hundred, depending on the propagator's requirements. If needed, a rose can be identified by taking a sample to the field where others grow and comparing it. Moje Hammarberg lives with us as a small hedge nestled among rows of similar roses.

Moje has several distinguishing characteristics. The center of the opening flower is slightly more pointed than most. Its leaves are larger than the old cultivar Hansa and slightly smaller than its near twin Magnifica, and the bush is somewhat more compact than its look-alike.

This rose makes a lovely medium-sized hedge that will

Magnifica is another excellent mauve *rugosa* with a slightly larger flower.

bloom and then rebloom. The flowers are plentiful, well formed, very fragrant and less susceptible to thrips and midges than others. It produces hips, so it is useful to those who make rose hip jam or tea. As well, it roots easily

All in all, Moje Hammarberg is a flower workhorse with hardiness, productivity, saturated color and rich fragrance.

MORDEN CENTENNIAL

Hardiness Zone: 3b
Introduced: 1980
Origin: Marshall, Canada
Parentage: Prairie Princess
× (White Bouquet × (J.W. Fargo
× Assiniboine))
Height: 4 ft. (1.25 m)
Fragrance: ff

This Canadian rose is a treasure. Morden Centennial's bush is very vigorous and upright-growing, with healthy deep green foliage. In our garden it suffers winter injury when temperatures fall below −22°F (−30°C), but even when the tops are killed back, the base rebounds and produces very double pink blooms of near-perfect symmetry. The veins that run through the petals are a deeper pink than the surrounding tissue, giving the blossoms a rather unique look.

Morden Centennial has a pleasant, albeit light, perfume, and it roots relatively well from cuttings. The large flowers are arranged in clusters that could make an ideal centerpiece for your table.

There are several other roses in the Parkland Series that bear mentioning. Morden Belle is a prolific bloomer with medium-pink blossoms, and Morden Fireglow is a rich orange-red double that reblooms. The weakness of these cultivars in our area was their propensity for blackspot. In a drier climate these roses perform better and are well worth growing.

MUSICIAN

Hardiness Zone: 2b
Introduced: 1953
Origin: Wright, Canada
Parentage: Hansa × Hazeldean
Height: 5 ft. (1.5 m)
Fragrance: f

From the beginning of my rose collecting days I held a burning desire to acquire this rose. It was said to be a bicolor blend of pink and yellow, and very hardy. The name was intriguing and, best of all, there was a story.

It seems Musician had, to all intents, been lost. The original plants had died, and no others could be found. Eventually, one was discovered growing in the garden of a man in Toronto, Ontario. The story goes that he refused anyone who wanted to take cuttings from his plant. It seemed he liked the feeling of having the only one. But rosarians can be persistent. Apparently, someone was eventually successful, and this very rare rose made it into the hands of a small group of rose propagators and growers.

My initial reaction to the first blooms on my small plant was a blend of laughter and disappointment. Laughter because over the years I had created a certain image of what this rose would look like, and the reality was wildly different. Disappointment because I found the colors muddy. On rainy days the petals would quickly saturate, and when the sun arrived they would harden and not allow the blossom to open properly, or at all.

The inclusion of this rose, despite my early assessment, is actually because of its uniqueness. The unusual pastels resemble washes of paint on silk. The bush appears to sucker little, and the stems seem to arrange themselves in horizontal layers, making the plant as wide as it is tall. Musician is also hardy to somewhere just south of the Arctic Circle. And, of course, there is the story: the nearly extinct rose that was rescued from its bondage to be made available to the world again.

NICHOLAS

Hardiness Zone: 3b
Introduced: 1996
Origin: Svejda, Canada
Parentage: B08 (A15 × D36)
   × L03 (*Rosa kordesii* × Applejack)
Height: 5 ft. (1.5 m)
Fragrance: f

We were lucky enough to see this rose bloom in our nursery when it was still an unnamed seedling. It had been sent to us by Agriculture Canada as a possible future release in the Explorer Series program. Little N06, as it was then known, immediately caught our attention.

The bush we deemed smallish, with shiny green foliage that rarely harbors disease.

The buds resemble tiny tops, and they spin open to reveal a semidouble flower that is a unique shade of scarlet red. Nicholas blooms in waves through the entire season. Although neat and compact we soon discovered the plant could easily grow higher than we first imagined. This rose does not have much scent, but its small stature and brilliant color make it a valuable addition to the family of hardy roses. It is also very easy to root.

PARFUM DE L'HAY

Hardiness Zone: 3b
Introduced: 1901
Origin: Gravereaux, France
Parentage: (*Rosa damascena*
   × General Jacqueminot)
   × *Rosa rugosa*
Height: 5 ft. (1.5 m)
Fragrance: ffff

The garden would be a diminished place without Parfum de l'Hay. It is a perfect blend of the roses that went into its genetic makeup. It has the rugged constitution of the *rugosa* rose and the color and form of the Damask rose and the Hybrid Perpetual.

The bush is vigorous and upright with deep olive-green foliage that is very resistant to disease, though you might see a bit of blackspot on the older foliage. It is well armed with prickles, but in keeping with the rose's reputation for pain and pleasure, the flowers are spectacular — large, fragrant and easy on the eyes. Grand globular buds burst open to a handsome double form of reddish-purple. Few roses can vie with Parfum de l'Hay for fragrance. It is sweet like its *rugosa* parent, but rounded out with the delicacy of the Damask rose.

Luckily for the gardener this rose will perform throughout the season, though it will not bloom as heavily as many modern roses. We would not want to be without this old but ever-vibrant plant.

Parfum de l'Hay is somewhat finicky to root. Use the smaller lateral stems and take them just as the first buds appear. We usually successfully root about 60 percent of the cuttings we take.

PERSIAN YELLOW

Hardiness Zone: 3b
Introduced: 1835
Origin: unknown, Southwestern Asia
Parentage: *Rosa foetida persiana*
Height: 4 ft. (1.25 m)
Fragrance: ff

This very hardy bush is generally upright with a tendency to sprawl as it ages. Its branches are somewhat thin and a bit wayward. It is not totally ungainly, and as it matures, this rose assumes a fairly full and impressive stature. This is definitely one rose to prune with restraint. Its flowers arise from the old wood, so drastic spring pruning will severely limit your blooms. As well, this rose does not seem to respond well to heavy pruning, and continued aggressive pruning may kill the plant.

Persian Yellow is a cultivar you will almost undoubtedly need to treat with a fungicide such as wettable sulfur if you want to keep the bush healthy. If not treated, it will drop most of its leaves shortly after flowering. Areas with humid summers will be particularly affected. Those in drier areas will find Persian Yellow fairly easy to grow. It even does well in poor sandy soils.

Persian Yellow is extremely difficult to root from softwood cuttings, particularly if any blackspot is present on the cuttings. Use cuttings taken as flowering begins and avoid over misting. It is virtually always budded or grafted. Plant such roses deep, so that the cultivar can form its own roots in time.

I have included this rose because of its historical importance. To be honest we no longer grow this rose at our nursery.

Virtually every yellow rose can trace its color back to this double form of *Rosa foetida*. Originally found in southwestern Asia, *Rosa foetida*'s origin is shrouded in the mists of ancient history. Around 1835 this double form appeared and was soon introduced into European and North American gardens. Rose breeders, including the French firm Pernet-Duchet, used it for its rich, golden color and double form. As well as transmitting its color, Persian Yellow has contributed its susceptibility to blackspot to the genetic "soup" of modern roses. But it's hard to complain about spots when the alternative is a world without yellow roses.

The flowers of Persian Yellow appear in late spring and continue for three or four weeks. The form is globular. The fragrance is light and unusual, although I do not think it fetid, as many have suggested.

PIERETTE PAVEMENT

Hardiness Zone: 3a
Introduced: 1987
Origin: Uhl, Germany
Parentage: unknown, *Rosa rugosa* hybrid
Height: 7 ft. (2 m)
Fragrance: fff

Pierette Pavement is one of the Pavement Series, introduced from Europe in the late 1980s. The choice of "pavement" as a marketing name for this group of roses is unfortunate. It gives one the impression that these are low ground-cover roses, which is hardly the case. The name was chosen, I would guess, because they spread very rapidly, making them ideal for covering banks or creating masses quickly.

Despite the name, these *Rosa rugosa* hybrids have proven to be good selections. If you are a fan of "big," then you will enjoy growing Pierette Pavement. The medium magenta pink flowers are very large and their fragrance is sweetly reminiscent of cloves. The foliage never shows signs of disease, making it even more attractive where low maintenance is a priority. Cuttings also root very easily.

PINK PAVEMENT

Hardiness Zone: 2b
Introduced: 1985
Origin: Uhl, Germany
Parentage: unknown, *Rosa rugosa* hybrid
Height: 6 ft. (1.75 m)
Fragrance: fff

I am a bud man. I love the look of a rose as it first emerges. With luck it is unsullied and fresh. Those hours between dawn — when the waiting bud starts to expand — and midday — when it has opened fully, advertising its readiness to be pollinated — are when the flower is at its height of elegance.

The buds on Pink Pavement are uniquely pointed, a feature only those who look closely might notice. Also the color is distinctively pink, as opposed to the more mauve-pink of the so-called pink

rugosa roses. It is an effective plant for road medians or steep banks, as its spreading nature is ideal for erosion control, and it is very salt tolerant and hardy.

Pink Pavement is also easy to root when cuttings are taken as the first flowers appear.

PRISTINE PAVEMENT

Hardiness Zone: 2b
Introduced: 1990
Origin: Baum, Germany
Parentage: unknown, *Rosa rugosa* hybrid
Height: 5 ft. (1.5 m)
Fragrance: fff

The original name of this rose, Schneeberg, means "snow mountain" or "snow hill," and in time it can form a fair-sized hill of snowy blooms. For us the standout feature of Pristine

Pavement is the bud. It is pointed and has the faintest hint of pink, especially in cool weather. Once open it becomes a pristine white semidouble with messy petals.

The bush is extremely healthy with virtually no disease or insect damage. It will spread if allowed, but is not as aggressive as some of its pavement kin. Although continual wet weather may saturate the petals and create balling, it seems to have better resistance to this problem than many.

It is an easy rose to root if cuttings are taken early in the flowering period.

PURPLE PAVEMENT

Hardiness Zone: 2b
Introduced: 1983
Origin: Baum, Germany
Parentage: *Rosa arvensis* × *Rosa rugosa*
Height: 7 ft. (2 m)
Fragrance: fff

Purple Pavement, also known as Rotesmeer, is a rapidly spreading plant that is ideal for covering large areas. The rampant nature of this cultivar makes it unsuitable for a flower bed but great for developed sites where massing is desired, or perhaps in the median of a road where it is kept in check by curbs. We use this rose to cover a large bank, which eliminates the need for weeding or mowing.

The leaves are typical of a *rugosa* rose, with a glossy sheen that is an indication of this variety's unparalleled health. The flowers are among the deepest colored

of the *Rosa rugosa* hybrids, being deep reddish-purple with shapely unfurling buds. The fragrance is strong and sweet.

The early flowers are often afflicted by thrips, which create

misshapen petals, although this does little to detract from the sheer exuberance of the blooms, which continue until late in the season. Purple Pavement is easy to root any time during the first flowering.

QUEEN OF DENMARK

Hardiness Zone: 4a
Introduced: 1826
Origin: Booth, Denmark
Parentage: *Rosa alba* × unknown
   Rosa damascena
Height: 4 ft. (1.25 m)
Fragrance: ffff

The Queen of Denmark (also known as Königin von Dänemark) belongs to the royal family of old garden roses. Many rose fanciers have a special place in their gardens for this most attractive and reliable cultivar. Its short fat buds are nearly encased by long filigreed sepals. They open to reveal artfully arranged petals so numerous they appear to swirl around the small central button of stamens. Though the flower flattens, its outer petals act to hold everything in place, so that it never becomes loose and disheveled. The pure pink tone of this rose is deeper than most of the *Rosa alba* group, fading gently to soft pink before the petals drop. The fragrance that emanates from the Queen befits nobility and is one more reason for the continuing popularity of this old rose.

This rose makes a most attractive floral arrangement. There is something about the Queen that sets it apart and plucks at the heart strings. I always say I have no favorites, but this might be my desert island choice.

Generally, it is a pleasure to prune the *alba* roses because they are not as prickly as most shrub roses, but be sure to put on your gloves for this one. Its stems, although not as vicious as those of the *rugosa* roses, make you pay for the dismemberment you inflict on them. Beware that you don't go too hard on the plants as they only bloom off of old wood, so heavy pruning will diminish the display. The bush is a nicely shaped tall mound clothed in handsome gray-green foliage that can be bowed with the weight of its large flowers.

Although relatively easy to root, care should be taken to collect the cuttings just as flowering commences. Leafhoppers love the foliage, so try to use cuttings that are free from injury. The Queen is a bit fussier than some, but if the conditions are good you can usually root 75 percent of your cuttings.

Like all *albas*, this rose flowers but once. However, the flowers that crown this distinguished rose are the highlights of a most glorious reign. Long live the Queen.

RAUBRITTER

Hardiness Zone: 4a
Introduced: 1936
Origin: Kordes, Germany
Parentage: Daisy Hill × Solarium
Height: 3 ft. (1 m) or more
Fragrance: fff

A rose with large clusters of pure pink globular flowers that put you in mind of Lilliputian peonies — Raubritter is absolutely enchanting and unlike anything else in the garden. In a warmer climate this rose can grow quite a bit larger than I have suggested, but in our garden it remains fairly low and squat with slender branching. What is perhaps the most endearing quality is its scent. It reminds me of freshly ground pepper without the sneeze. It is one of the latest roses to begin blooming and lasts into late summer.

We have been surprised by the hardiness of this rose as well as its resistance to disease. This is another of the fabulous line of introductions by the storied Kordes family of Germany. The world of hardy roses would be a much poorer place if it had not been for their insistence on breeding for hardiness and health.

Cuttings root relatively easily if taken just as blossoms begin.

SARAH VAN FLEET

Hardiness Zone: 4a
Introduced: 1926
Origin: Van Fleet, USA
Parentage: *Rosa rugosa* Thunb. × My Maryland
Height: 4 ft. (1.25 m)
Fragrance: fff

Many people have told me they don't grow shrub roses because the plants don't bloom long enough. This attitude is, sadly, a widely held one, mainly because many of the better cultivars are not widely available to the public. Many of these roses are new in the nursery trade, and it takes many years to get enough out in the landscape to create a demand. Until recently there has been little incentive for the nursery trade to propagate shrub roses. The public seemed uninterested in the shrubs. New trends in gardening, however, have dramatically changed the situation.

Cultivars such as Sarah Van Fleet will go a long way toward revising people's perception of shrub roses. It is a later bloomer that gives a perpetual show of fragrant, clear pink, semidouble blooms. While not quite as hardy as some of its *Rosa rugosa* relatives, Sarah Van Fleet does very well in our garden, even in the worst years, killing back only the top half of its vigorous, upright shoots. In warmer areas this rose will form a tall shrub. Under more northern conditions it will stay somewhat smaller, but each year's shoots are remarkably tall.

This rose does not set hips. It does suffer from a bit of blackspot on the lower leaves, and I have seen a touch of mildew in damp conditions. I have read that this cultivar is inclined to rust, although I have not seen any on our plants. Although this makes the plant sound like a mass of disease, we have found it generally quite healthy and easy to root from softwood cuttings.

SCHNEEZWERG

Hardiness Zone: 2b
Introduced: 1912
Origin: Lambert, Germany
Parentage: *Rosa rugosa* × *Rosa beggeriana*
Height: 3 ft. (1 m)
Fragrance: fff

From late spring until hard frost this tough and adaptable bush sends forth innumerable small pure white blossoms. As each semidouble bloom opens, a center of deep yellow stamens adds a cheerful accent to the flower.

Schneezwerg's lustrous, healthy foliage amply demonstrates the disease resistance so common to the *rugosa* roses. It is lower growing than nearly any other *rugosa* rose and its density makes it a good low hedge. With annual attention to shaping and thinning, a hedge of Schneezwerg could be a valuable addition to your garden.

To all these attributes, add a sweet and powerful fragrance and a hardiness that is virtually unmatched in the rose world. Although still more popular in Europe than in North America, Schneezwerg remains a valuable white *rugosa* rose. Several modern breeders have used it to create new cultivars. It was used for many crosses by Felicitas Svejda of Agriculture Canada to produce some of the Explorer Series of roses, including Henry Hudson.

Schneezwerg gives you all the beauty of a fresh snowfall without the bother of having to shovel it. This rose is easy to root from softwood cuttings taken just at flowering. Suckers can be used as well.

STANWELL PERPETUAL

Hardiness Zone: 3b
Introduced: 1838
Origin: Lee, UK
Parentage: assumed to be *Rosa damascena bifera* × *Rosa spinosissima*
Height: 5 ft. (1.5 m)
Fragrance: ffff

It is by listening to the advice of others that we learn. In one of my early correspondences with a rose grower, I was told that I had to acquire Stanwell Perpetual. My friend assured me that it would soon become one of my favorites. And so it has.

The story of this rose is one of serendipity. In the town of Stanwell in England a seedling rose appeared, some say in a hedgerow. Nearby were growing a Scotch rose, noted for its small compound foliage and superb hardiness, and a bush of *Rosa damascena*, known as the Four Seasons Damask rose. The latter rose, as the name suggests, is a repeat bloomer. The foundling had the hardiness of the Scotch rose and its nine leaflet foliage, but with the reblooming ability of the Damask. It is our great blessing that this rose was recognized and introduced.

The flower is double, with the old-time charm of the Damask rose. Its soft, blush-pink blossoms cover the plant in late spring, and from then on a regular procession of flowers appears on this gracefully arching bush. The foliage is a deep green and, aside from a natural purplish discoloration, is unmarred by disease.

Although usually budded, Stanwell can be rooted if the cuttings are not kept too wet. Expect a small plant at first with thin, wiry stems. You can also find suckers on older plants that can provide a few new plants. No matter the method, within a few years you will be thankful for this random gift from the universe.

Stanwell Perpetual never fails to make me stop, bend down and smell the roses. It asks very little of us and gives so much. It pays to take advice.

WILLIAMS' DOUBLE

Hardiness Zone: 2b
Introduced: 1820
Origin: Williams, UK
Parentage: thought to be *Rosa spinosissima* L. × *Rosa foetida* Herrm.
Height: 4 ft. (1.25 m)
Fragrance: ff

Williams' Double is an old rose that is known across the northern latitudes of the globe by many different names. A few include Old Double Scots rose, Namdalsrosen and Hoog's Straw Colored, among others. It is very popular in Scandinavia — a good indication of its winter hardiness.

This cultivar is another of the small pool of tough yellow roses that can be counted on to survive −40°F (−40°C) and come back with a spectacular display of butter-yellow blossoms the following spring. Williams' Double is very similar in many respects to Harison's Yellow, though perhaps the flowers of Williams' Double have slightly fewer petals, although it's still a double.

We have found the bush as hardy as Hazeldean, another similar and equally tough fellow, but Williams' Double does not suffer from blackspot in our humid climate, whereas Hazeldean is often infected. It is slightly less apt to ball in wet weather but is still susceptible.

It is our experience that Williams' Double does not grow as tall as other Scotch roses. Perhaps this is due to the influence of its *Rosa foetida* genes. It does sucker like a Scotch rose. Certainly it gives one who tends this rose a source of highly desirable suckers to give to friends and fellow gardeners. Rooting this rose, as with many yellows, is not as dependable as others, but if cuttings are taken early and kept only as humid as necessary, a good crop can be raised this way.

9

LOW SHRUBS

Shrubs growing up to 3 ft. (1 m)

◄ The blooms of Campfire
morph from yellow to pink as
they age, giving the plant a
unique and enticing look.

CAMPFIRE

Hardiness Zone: 3b
Introduced: 2012
Origin: Dyck, Canada
Parentage: My Hero × Frontenac
Height: 3 ft. (1 m)
Fragrance: f

One could say that Campfire has caught on like wildfire. This rose was introduced by Agriculture Canada as one of the Canadian Artist Series. Its yellow and red coloration was said to resemble the tones of a campfire in a painting rendered by Tom Thomson, a famous painter of Canadian landscapes who was associated with the Group of Seven.

This is another rose that originated at the Morden Research and Development Centre in Manitoba. A cross was made using My Hero, a hardy red shrub rose bred by Ling and Twomey in 1993 and released by Bailey Nurseries as one of its Easy Elegance Series, and Frontenac,

an Explorer Series rose bred by Felicitas Svejda of Agriculture Canada that produces pink flowers continuously and is very hardy.

This new rose immediately caught the eye of everyone who walked the rows of seedlings and was soon selected and assigned the designation CA29. When the Canadian rose consortium committee met to choose a new introduction, it was the unanimous choice of the entire group, in part because of its unusual and captivating color, but also because it had shown good hardiness at all the testing stations.

This harlequin of a rose begins as a semidouble yellow with red-

dish edges, then ages to a deep rose-pink. Because it is continuously blooming, all stages of this transition are present, creating a multicolored visual feast. We have been told by countless people that this rose is their absolute favorite.

One characteristic that sets it apart from many hardy roses is its lack of suckering. This allows the bush to be put into beds without fear of it taking over, as many roses are wont to do. The rich green stems are very lightly armored and grow at a 45-degree angle, creating a bush that is as wide as it is tall.

At our site we experience some winter injury to the tops, but it robustly recovers and creates a show nearly unmatched. Even as hard frost arrives, the bush will be covered in blooms. At the Morden Research and Development Centre in Manitoba, where it was bred, it is reliably crown hardy.

This rose is extremely easy to root, with success rates nearing 100 percent if all proper conditions are met.

While most love to sit around a campfire at night admiring its flickering hues, I'm fairly certain you will find it just as pleasurable to sit around a bloom of Campfire in the daylight and enjoy its hot colors trembling in the breeze.

CANADA BLOOMS

Hardiness Zone: 4b
Introduced: 2014
Origin: Richer, Canada
Parentage: Secret × Astrid Lindgren
Height: 3 ft. (1 m)
Fragrance: ffff

We first saw Canada Blooms among a group of roses that we were testing for Agriculture Canada. The hope was that one or more of these seedlings would be suitable for the Canadian Artist Series. Its designation was CA28. When the first blossoms opened we were stunned by the size, the perfect symmetry, the sumptuous pink color and, most of all, the heady perfume. No rose in our collection can match the quality of its fragrance, one destined for the pots of some future perfumer who will distill and capture its essence. The aromas are deeply intoxicating but with no cloying sweetness — a sensuous perfume station you can install in your garden. This rose was introduced at the Canada Blooms garden show in Toronto, Ontario, and has gained a steady following since.

This is not a plant that fits the usual template. In our area it is a non-suckering upright plant with vigorous stems that are reminiscent of a long-stemmed greenhouse rose. Indeed, the single rose that sits atop the stem lasts longer than any other hardy rose I know. Where most fall apart within a day or two, Canada Blooms will last a week if picked just before opening.

This rose is not the hardiest of the selections. In our garden in Zone 4 it will often kill to near the ground, but it comes back to deliver what are the most prized of all blooms. A bit of extra protection in colder areas will help see this through the winter. Certainly in Zones 5 and warmer this rose will thrive and deliver flowers that will astound the eyes and delight the nose.

We have found Canada Blooms roots easily, though being more rose than leaf, cutting material is always in short supply. This is a rose that is best grown own rooted in colder areas. A budded rose might induce more vigor, but you could find the top killed and only the rootstock remaining after an open winter.

CARDINAL DE RICHELIEU

Hardiness Zone: 4a (possibly 3b)
Introduced: 1840
Origin: Parmentier, Belgium
Parentage: unknown, *Rosa gallica* hybrid
Height: 3 ft. (1 m)
Fragrance: ffff

This is a rose with an intense fragrance. We once used the petals to create a rose petal jam that was outstanding. Though not a jam you would generally use on toast, it is highly sought out by those who believe it will relieve menstrual cramps and can be used for other medical issues. This is a particularly important product in the Indian subcontinent. We enjoyed just taking a small dollop straight on the tongue and inhaling the essence of this rose.

This is one of the toughest of the *Rosa gallicas*, hardy to at least −35°F (−37°C). Its leaves may show some blackspot near the bottom of the bush, but this is never enough to mar the appearance of the plant. Cuttings taken early in the season root well. The plant will spread by suckers as it ages, and these provide an easy way to multiply your plant or to give one to a friend.

The namesake of this rose was Cardinal de Richelieu, a minister to Louis XIII of France in the 17th century. He is famous to some, infamous to others, but for our purposes the rose that sports the kind of deep purple that once embellished the robes of the cardinal will remain famous as long as roses are grown.

If you are a purple person, this elderly representative of the *Rosa gallica* tribe is for you. Its mum-like very double bloom is the quintessential purple among hardy roses. The globular buds open in early summer to form perfectly symmetrical flowers in profusion on a dense plant that usually grows not much higher than 3 ft. (1 m). Our bushes bloom for four to five weeks.

The last flowers on our plants exhibit a curious trait. Through the center of each flower a small stalk with a stunted version of another flower emerges. This process is called proliferation and, although not unique to Cardinal de Richelieu, this cultivar produces these aberrations with a regularity we have never seen elsewhere.

CELESTIAL

Hardiness Zone: 4a
Introduced: before 1848
Origin: unknown
Parentage: unknown, *Rosa alba* group
Height: 3 ft. (1 m)
Fragrance: fff

When you are in the business of selling plants, you realize how strongly people react to the emotional connotations of names. Give a dog of a plant a catchy name and it will sell . . . for a while. Ultimately, a plant's merits become its best advertisement and determine its staying power.

Celestial is a nurseryman's dream come true; for here is a name that conjures up images of heavenly choirs or colorful galaxies floating in space and a flower that actually lives up to these visions of ethereal beauty — a rose of the purest pink and the most delicate of textures. This fine and very old double form of the *Rosa alba* has remained popular for centuries.

These (dare I use the word) heavenly smelling roses are set on a very neat bush with bluish-green foliage. Though perhaps not for subarctic areas, most northern gardeners should have no trouble overwintering this carefree and rewarding rose or propagating it from softwood cuttings. It has been noted that this rose resents constant pruning back, so treat it gently. Every stem cut back reduces the floral display in the future.

CHAMPLAIN

Hardiness Zone: 4a
Introduced: 1982
Origin: Svejda, Canada
Parentage: (*Rosa kordesii* Wulff × (*Rosa laxa* × *Rosa spinosissima* L.)) × (Red Dawn × Suzanne)
Height: 3 ft. (1 m)
Fragrance: ff

Champlain is a hardy and ever-blooming rose. Once it begins, only the hard frosts can stop it. Although certainly not an ironclad hardy plant, it is a valuable addition to the northern garden. In our garden we often experience a good deal of dieback with Champlain, but we rarely lose a plant. When on its own roots it is able to spring back, even if killed to almost ground level.

Champlain's blooms are a velvety, rich deep red. In addition to its sumptuous color, this rose is entirely free of disease. It is exceedingly resistant to blackspot and mildew. What is even more exciting is that under outside growing conditions Champlain is virtually free of aphids. Many roses seem somewhat resistant to these pesky green sap suckers, but Champlain is truly exceptional. This would be a good parent for some hybridizer looking for insect resistance.

Under ideal conditions Champlain can grow quite large, but in outside northern conditions it is often lower in stature and makes an excellent bedding rose. If this cultivar has a fault, it is that the plant seems all bloom at the expense of foliage. With proper pruning, however, it forms a compact and useful garden subject.

It is extremely easy to root, although cuttings are often difficult to obtain in numbers due to the preponderance of flowers and paucity of vegetative wood.

CHARLES DE MILLS

Hardiness Zone: 3b
Introduced: before 1700
Origin: unknown, Netherlands
Parentage: unknown, *Rosa gallica* group
Height: 2.5 ft (0.75 m)
Fragrance: ffff

On a warm July day, I noticed a slightly exasperated-looking woman working her way purposefully through the garden. As I approached her to ask if I could help, she looked up and shouted, "Don't you have any double roses here?" I pointed out several roses near her that were double. "Oh, not that kind. I mean *really* double." I realized that this lady was looking not for a double rose but for what is called a quartered rose, one with so many petals that, lacking room, the flower seems to fold itself into four equal parts. I led her to Charles de Mills, and when she saw the large and extravagant blooms an instant calm spread across her face. "Now that's a rose," she lectured me.

Charles de Mills' flowers are a glowing blend of rich red and purple with the edges shading toward the deepest of pinks. Unlike many of the shrub roses it maintains an elegant cupped form even when fully open, and a bush covered with these large vibrant flowers forms an attractive centerpiece in any garden. Add to this the flower's sweet perfume, and it is not surprising that this is one of the most popular of the *Rosa gallicas*.

The deep green foliage is rarely bothered by disease, although the occasional blackspot will show up on older leaves or where air circulation is poor. The bush is a miniature forest of upright canes that will grow wider with time and whose outer suckers provide an easy way to create more plants. It is easy to root from cuttings as well.

MORDEN BLUSH

Hardiness Zone: 3b
Introduced: 1976
Origin: Marshall, Canada
Parentage: (Prairie Princess
    × Morden Amorette) × ((Prairie
    Princess × White Bouquet)
    × (*Rosa arkansana* × Assiniboine))
Height: 3 ft. (1 m)
Fragrance: ff

Although bred in Morden, Manitoba, which is in hardiness Zone 3b, Morden Blush is a bit tender at our site. However, it would be unfair not to include this lovely rose. Even when injured by winter it bounces back and produces a wealth of flowers for the entire growing season. And what flowers!

The large double blooms are the softest of pinks and of exquisite form. The bush is upright but low in stature. Given a protected site it will reward you with copious clusters of blooms. They are good cut flowers as well.

Morden Blush cuttings root easily.

MORDEN RUBY

Hardiness Zone: 3b
Introduced: 1977
Origin: Marshall, Canada
Parentage: Fire King × (J.W.
    Fargo × Assiniboine)
Height: 3 ft. (1 m)
Fragrance: f

When you see our Morden Ruby roses, you might think pixies inhabit our garden. Each time one of the blossoms opens, it looks as if little fairies have splattered the deep pink petals with dabs of red paint, creating a fascinating spotted pattern that should make many an abstract painter envious. Interestingly, we later learned that the cultivar released as Morden Ruby is a solid red sport of the original spotted seedling. The plants we received were spotted and we had assumed that was the true cultivar. Now some of our plants have reverted back to the solid red color — seems they can't make up their minds.

Nevertheless, both flowers are beautiful and allow us to forgive the plant's weaknesses. Morden Ruby is rather open, so pruning it back in spring will help keep the plant denser. It is also a bit too susceptible to blackspot for our liking. However, a few sprays of sulfur or turning a blind eye make this all-too-common weakness disappear. Morden Ruby has an important point in its favor: the blossoms we cherish so highly come in several waves throughout the summer, so we can gaze at these fascinating flowers for many months.

Morden Ruby is fairly easy to root, but cuttings often drop leaves shortly after rooting. Be sure there is no blackspot on your cuttings.

MORDEN SNOW BEAUTY

Hardiness Zone: 3b
Introduced: 2001
Origin: Collicutt, Canada
Parentage: ((Adelaide Hoodless
× *Rosa arkansana* Porter)
× Mount Shasta) × (Prairie
Princess × Morden Amorette)
Height: 2.5 ft. (0.75 m)
Fragrance: ff

Morden Snow Beauty should be better known. Perhaps some of its obscurity is because it is not a double rose, and white is not the most popular color, but it's a cultivar with charm, health and hardiness in spades.

The bush is quite low and is often wider than high. We never see any disease affecting its glossy green foliage. The flowers have anywhere from eight to 14 petals, and the blossoms arrive in small clusters. The center of each flower is green with yellow stamens. It is a simple yet refined bloom.

This is a wonderful rose for containers or where a low bedding rose that does not sucker is required. Of course white goes with anything, making this a great plant for color combinations. Best of all its snow-white flowers will keep blooming throughout the season.

Morden Snow Beauty is easy to root if cuttings are taken early in the flowering season.

PRAIRIE JOY

Hardiness Zone: 3b
Introduced: 1990
Origin: Colicutt and Marshall, Canada
Parentage: Prairie Princess × Morden Cardinette
Height: 3 ft. (1 m)
Fragrance: f

Some of the earliest improved hardy roses were bred at Agriculture Canada's Morden Research and Development Centre in Morden, Manitoba. The strength of these introductions has been good flower form. Prairie Joy has both excellent form and a small stature, making it an ideal low hedge plant. It is also a prolific bloomer and has good hardiness.

Many of the Morden introductions are prone to blackspot in humid areas. Prairie Joy has better resistance than most of the earlier releases, but we do recommend sulfur sprays to prevent blackspot from marring the otherwise glossy deep green foliage. The semidouble flowers start cupped, then open, and the petals are a clear bright pink. The blooms, which have little fragrance, appear in clusters until the season's end. Cuttings root readily and will turn into vigorous plants quickly.

ROSA MUNDI

Hardiness Zone: 3b
Introduced: ca. 1580
Origin: unknown, Europe
Parentage: color sport of *Rosa gallica officinalis*
Height: 2.5 ft. (0.75 m)
Fragrance: fff

No two flowers of Rosa Mundi ever look the same. A spectacular display of color chaos, each bloom has a different combination of red, pink and white striping. I love to pick dozens of blooms and float them in a large bowl of water, marveling at the uniqueness of each flower. Rosa Mundi is one of the harlequins of the rose world. It has enchanted the world since the 16th century and, I dare say, will continue to do so for centuries to come.

In order to remain in the horticultural pantheon, a rose has to be tough. Rosa Mundi fits the bill. It is among the hardiest of the *Rosa gallica* group and will thrive with little attention for decades. The matte green foliage is not very susceptible to blackspot, but this rose can suffer from mildew late in the season. Personally, I never pay much heed to it as the flowers are usually done by this point, and it does not seem to cause the bush undue harm. As with most *Rosa gallicas*, the fragrance of Rosa Mundi is powerful.

It can be easily rooted from cuttings, but the propagator should be wary, as this rose can revert back to the single soft red color found in the Apothecary rose (*Rosa gallica officinalis*), from which it arose as a color sport.

SIMON FRASER

Hardiness Zone: 3b
Introduced: 1992
Origin: Svejda, Canada
Parentage: ((Bonanza × Arthur Bell) × (Red Dawn × Suzanne)) × ((*Rosa kordesii* o.p. × *Rosa kordesii* o.p.) × Champlain)
Height: 3 ft. (1 m)
Fragrance: f

The most common color in roses is pink. There seems to be no end to the various shades available, yet Simon Fraser has added yet another subtle hue to the pink palette. This pink is somewhere between shrimp and salmon. The blooms themselves are very simple. In fact, the first blooms you see on the bush may be single, but as it matures the number of petals increases to 10 or so.

Like other Explorer Series roses, Simon Fraser has exceedingly healthy foliage and uncommon hardiness. The plant is quite small and boasts one of the most extravagant displays of bloom in its class. Its glossy foliage is nearly hidden by the first flush of bloom in early summer. From then until frost there are always plenty of pink petals to draw attention to this attractive newcomer. Propagators will find this rose easy to root when cuttings are taken early in the flowering season.

SNOWDRIFT

Hardiness Zone: 4a
Introduced: 2007
Origin: Lim, USA
Parentage: Sexy Rexy × Carefree Delight
Height: 3 ft. (1 m)
Fragrance: f

Bailey Nurseries, located near the Mississippi River in central Minnesota, is one of America's premier growers of ornamental plants. Among its many accomplishments is the introduction of several excellent disease-resistant roses. Snowdrift is a fine example, and one of the hardiest.

It is a dense, compact plant, well-endowed with glossy, deep green foliage. The plant does not sucker, making it a fine selection for the garden bed. Although in our garden in Zone 4 we experience dieback in a harsh winter, Snowdrift is quite tough and will bounce back quickly. We do see some blackspot on the foliage, but a well-grown plant should not suffer badly.

And then there are the flowers. They are double and the purest of whites. Their tight, somewhat mounded form reminds one of a mum. This plant is truly continuously blooming, and its cuttings root easily if taken as flowering commences.

To create a wonderful complementary flower bed, try combining Snowdrift with other strongly colored roses. We used this rose with the deep red Canadian Shield, and the result stopped traffic.

We owe a debt of gratitude to the breeder of this rose, Ping Lim. His work has helped add many fine selections to the growing stable of hardy ever-blooming roses.

STRIPED MOSS

Hardiness Zone: 4a
Introduced: 1888
Origin: Verdier, France
Parentage: sport of Shailer's White Moss
Height: 2.5 ft. (0.75 m)
Fragrance: ff

Humans seem to crave the unusual in nature. In the gardening world we raise curious dwarfs, plants with twisted stems or foliage, and trees and shrubs with oddly colored leaves and flowers. For this reason roses such as Striped Moss (called *Oeillet Panaché* in French) are still found growing in our gardens, as this is indeed an odd rose.

The flowers are double, cupped and open flat. The white petals, heavily streaked with random stripes of deep and lighter pink, create an effect both startling and intriguing. Among striped roses, Striped Moss is one of the hardiest, reasonably easy to root and therefore of interest to northern growers. It is also blessed with good fragrance and the interesting fuzziness associated with the Moss roses. This rose can be affected by blackspot, so prevention with a fungicide such as wettable sulfur is wise.

The bush is small and upright with both stems and buds well mossed. It is well suited for an intimate corner in the garden, where the sun can warm its branches and give brilliance to the blossoms of this lovely oddity.

THE FAIRY

Hardiness Zone: 4b
Introduced: 1932
Origin: Bentall, UK
Parentage: Paul Crampel
   × Lady Gay
Height: 3 ft. (1 m)
Fragrance: f

The miniature roses (hybrids of *Rosa polyantha*) hold a special place in the rose world. Their diminutive stature, accompanied by their prolific flowering ability, make them highly sought after as potted plants and edging plants. Unfortunately for northern gardeners, most of the miniatures are tender and cannot survive outdoors in cold climates. There are a few exceptions, and one of the most notable is one of the older miniatures.

The Fairy is still popular because it is a beautiful soft pink and, once in bloom, is never out of bloom until it freezes. Another reason is the tenacity of this small plant. It survives where others wither and die. When exposed to temperatures below –22°F (–30°C) without snow cover, the stems may kill back to near the ground, but even in these situations the root system will send up new shoots in the spring.

Given a protected site, The Fairy will provide years of satisfaction. The tiny double blooms come in clusters so prolific that the bush resembles a giant bouquet. Although it is generally healthy, you can expect some blackspot in humid areas, so you may want to consider sprays of sulfur to prevent infection. The Fairy is easy to root from cuttings.

TUSCANY

Hardiness Zone: 4a (possibly 3b)
Introduced: ca. 1500
Origin: unknown, possibly Italy
Parentage: unknown, possibly a
Rosa gallica natural mutation
Height: 3 ft. (1 m)
Fragrance: ffff

Planting many of the shrub roses is akin to starting a raspberry patch. Roses are, after all, a type of bramble. They spread by underground stems that run outward and pop up several feet from where they started. Older canes will often die out to be replaced by new suckers. If you dig up roses, you will frequently be shocked at the lack of roots supporting the tops. There are often very few fibrous roots.

Tuscany is a low suckering plant in this vein. Having said this, I have seen this rose grow up through a shrub, attaining a height far greater than an open-grown plant. The blossoms on this rose are as decorative as the finest velvet — soft and in a shade of purple as rich and deep as a royal robe. These same flowers are also splendidly endowed with superb perfume. Tuscany is one of the very hardiest of the *Rosa gallica* group and is also one of the oldest, having been cherished by nobles and commoners for centuries.

In the early 19th century a slightly larger version with a few more petals was introduced as Tuscany Superba, a seedling of Tuscany bred by Thomas Rivers and Sons Ltd, sometime before 1837.

Tuscany roots easily and can be propagated by the many suckers that will appear.

10 GROUND COVERS

Procumbent or ground-hugging shrubs

◀ The low-lying Bassino starts
to flower later in the season
than most, but it will bloom
continuously until frost.

BASSINO

There are few true ground-cover roses. There are spreading roses that can act as ground covers, but these are usually much taller plants. Bassino never rises far above the ground. Its long lax stems bend of their own weight and that of the numerous five-petaled bright red blossoms that arrange themselves along them. The petals are glossy and catch the light.

Bassino survives at our site, thought we usually have to cut back many of the winter-injured long stems that formed the year before. This often leaves the crown and several short stems that grow in all directions. By summer they erupt once again and grace the edges of the bed with their glowing color. Each plant will cover 3 ft. (1 m) or more in width, but only grow to about 1 ft. (0.25 m) tall. It is important to find an own-rooted plant, as budded plants will be more upright.

This is one of the last roses to come into bloom, but once it does it will repeat in waves through the summer and into fall. Dead-heading old blooms will speed the process. As you go about your task you can admire the wavy edges of the flowers and the deep golden stamens that add visual delight to this lowly plant.

Bassino roots very easily from cuttings.

Hardiness Zone: 4b
Introduced: 1988
Origin: Kordes, Germany
Parentage: Sea Foam
× Red Max Graf
Height: 1 ft. (0.25 m)
Fragrance: f

MAX GRAF

Hardiness Zone: 4a
Introduced: 1919
Origin: Bowditch, USA
Parentage: *Rosa rugosa*
   × *Rosa wichuraiana*
Height: 1.5 ft. (0.5 m)
Fragrance: ff

This rose is vitally important in the historical development of many of our newest and best hardy shrub roses. Discovered in Connecticut by James Bowditch, this rose came to the attention of Wilhelm Kordes of Germany. He saved a seed from a chance fruit on his bush, and the seedling that resulted had good hardiness and a remarkable resistance to disease. He named it *Rosa kordesii*. Subsequent crosses using this new species resulted in many important hardy, healthy cultivars. Later, the breeder Felicitas Svejda of Agriculture Canada used these descendants of Max Graf to introduce black-spot resistance into the Explorer Series of roses.

Although not commonly seen in gardens, the original Max Graf can be useful to the northern gardener. Not only is it fairly hardy and healthy, but it also has a low branching structure that makes it a good ground cover. Its lax stems stretch outward, bending down from their own weight. As each successive layer covers the previous layers, a fairly dense low bush is created that is attractive and effective. The downside of this habit is that pruning can be an onerous task, particularly if there is winter injury throughout the tangle of branches.

Just because the flower is single and nonrecurrent, we should not dismiss it. Surrounding a prominent center of deep yellow stamens are five petals of clear, satiny pink that are delightfully, if lightly, scented. Even when not in flower the healthy sheen of the leaves and the long, arching, fresh green branches add beauty and texture to the garden.

Max Graf is very easy to root from cuttings and will also layer well.

REPENS ALBA

Repens Alba, also known as *Rosa paulii*, is a fascinating rose and one of the only true creeping roses that can be grown in the north. For us, this rose was an interesting lesson in the difference between budded and own-rooted plants. When we first received Repens Alba it was budded onto *Rosa multiflora* roots. I grew it the first year and was disappointed that it was not a true ground cover as I had hoped. It seemed to grow upward and then gradually arch outward, like a lazy fountain. We took cuttings. The next summer I was walking through the beds and came upon what looked like sinuous snakes on the ground. I had never seen a rose like it. I quickly backtracked to the sign and could hardly believe that this was the same plant that I had brought in. The *multiflora* root had caused the

plant to thrust upward, whereas these own-rooted plants never left the soil's surface. The two plants, alike in every respect but their roots, behaved in two completely different manners. This difference points to the importance of knowing what kind of plant you have, for their growth pattern can be significantly altered by budding them on a rootstock.

While this rose does not attain any height, it certainly does not lack vigor. It will grow rapidly and fill a good-sized area with its long, snaky shoots. Take care handling these stems, as their prickles can inflict serious damage to the unwary. In early summer large buds appear on the ends of the healthy and heavily textured foliage. They open to large star-shaped, pure white single blooms. The narrower-than-usual petals converge in the center, where

Hardiness Zone: 3b
Introduced: ca. 1903
Origin: Paul, UK
Parentage: unknown, assumed to be *Rosa arvensis* × *Rosa rugosa*
Height: less than 1 ft. (0.25 m)
Fragrance: fff

a sunburst of golden stamens completes the simple beauty of this flower with delicate elegance. The rose's sweet fragrance and colorful display of yellow and orange foliage in the fall help to make up for the fleeting season of this most useful plant.

Although thought of as a ground cover, Repens Alba could make a very interesting climber or rambler if tied to a trellis or fence. Just be sure to wear a thick pair of leather gloves when doing the tying.

The rose roots and layers easily.

APPENDIX

Canada's Extreme Minimum Temperature Zones

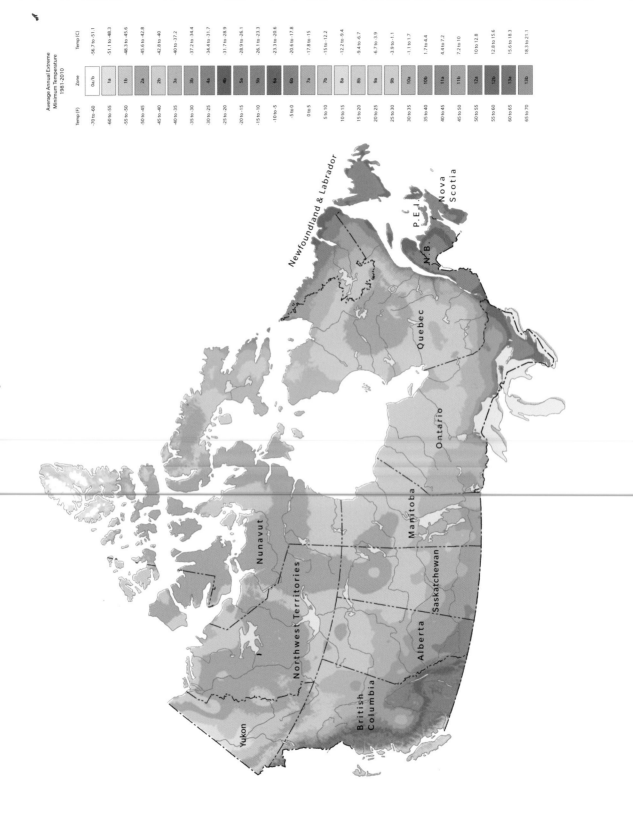

Average Annual Extreme Minimum Temperature 1981-2010

Temp (F)	Zone	Temp (C)
-70 to -60	0a/b	-56.7 to -51.1
-60 to -55	1a	-51.1 to -48.3
-55 to -50	1b	-48.3 to -45.6
-50 to -45	2a	-45.6 to -42.8
-45 to -40	2b	-42.8 to -40
-40 to -35	3a	-40 to -37.2
-35 to -30	3b	-37.2 to -34.4
-30 to -25	4a	-34.4 to -31.7
-25 to -20	4b	-31.7 to -28.9
-20 to -15	5a	-28.9 to -26.1
-15 to -10	5b	-26.1 to -23.3
-10 to -5	6a	-23.3 to -20.6
-5 to 0	6b	-20.6 to -17.8
0 to 5	7a	-17.8 to -15
5 to 10	7b	-15 to -12.2
10 to 15	8a	-12.2 to -9.4
15 to 20	8b	-9.4 to -6.7
20 to 25	9a	-6.7 to -3.9
25 to 30	9b	-3.9 to -1.1
30 to 35	10a	-1.1 to 1.7
35 to 40	10b	1.7 to 4.4
40 to 45	11a	4.4 to 7.2
45 to 50	11b	7.2 to 10
50 to 55	12a	10 to 12.8
55 to 60	12b	12.8 to 15.6
60 to 65	13a	15.6 to 18.3
65 to 70	13b	18.3 to 21.1

USDA Plant Hardiness Zone Map

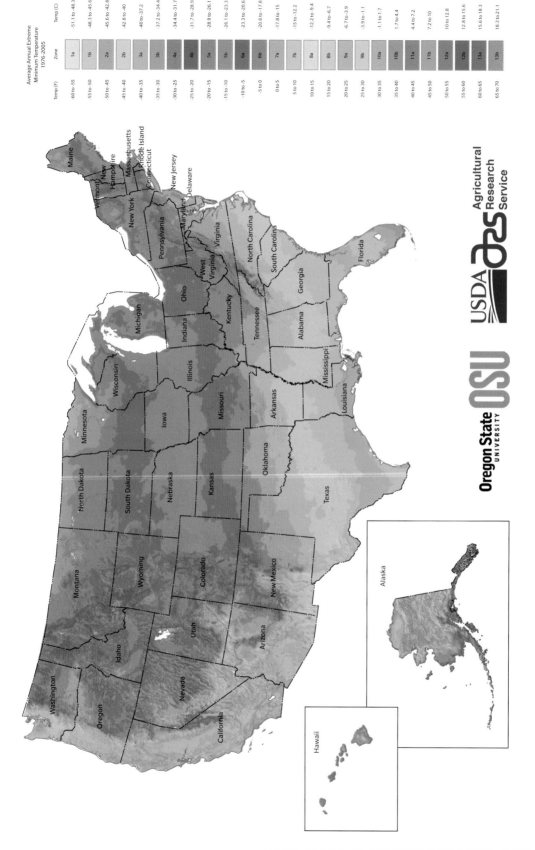

Average Annual Extreme Minimum Temperature 1976-2005		
Temp (F)	Zone	Temp (C)
-60 to -55	1a	-51.1 to -48.3
-55 to -50	1b	-48.3 to -45.6
-50 to -45	2a	-45.6 to -42.8
-45 to -40	2b	-42.8 to -40
-40 to -35	3a	-40 to -37.2
-35 to -30	3b	-37.2 to -34.4
-30 to -25	4a	-34.4 to -31.7
-25 to -20	4b	-31.7 to -28.9
-20 to -15	5a	-28.9 to -26.1
-15 to -10	5b	-26.1 to -23.3
-10 to -5	6a	-23.3 to -20.6
-5 to 0	6b	-20.6 to -17.8
0 to 5	7a	-17.8 to -15
5 to 10	7b	-15 to -12.2
10 to 15	8a	-12.2 to -9.4
15 to 20	8b	-9.4 to -6.7
20 to 25	9a	-6.7 to -3.9
25 to 30	9b	-3.9 to -1.1
30 to 35	10a	-1.1 to 1.7
35 to 40	10b	1.7 to 4.4
40 to 45	11a	4.4 to 7.2
45 to 50	11b	7.2 to 10
50 to 55	12a	10 to 12.8
55 to 60	12b	12.8 to 15.6
60 to 65	13a	15.6 to 18.3
65 to 70	13b	18.3 to 21.1

Oregon State UNIVERSITY

USDA Agricultural Research Service

LIST OF HARDY CULTIVARS

The following cultivars are those believed sufficiently hardy to be grown in Zones 2 to 5. The cultivars chosen are those that are currently available in the nursery trade. There are countless other roses, many of excellent quality and value, but they are either difficult or impossible to obtain. I have relied upon the expertise of others to assign each cultivar to a species or category. Some roses might just as easily be put in other sections, as they are often the result of interspecific breeding and have characteristics common to both species.

The designation of color, form, fragrance and blooming time are from the results of my own observations and those of others in the field. Some of these are somewhat subjective, and differences may occur according to where a cultivar is grown and the care given to it. Hardiness designations are based on observation, information from reliable sources and a bit of educated guesswork. These hardiness ratings should be used merely as a guide to assist those choosing suitable roses for their area.

◀ There is no need for those living in cold climates to deny themselves roses. There are cultivars for every garden, like Prairie Peace, which can grow in Zone 2.

THE CULTIVARS	COLOR	FORM	HARDINESS ZONE	VIGOR	FRAGRANCE	SEASON	SUITABILITY FOR HEDGING	DISEASE SUSCEPTIBILITY	BREEDER	COUNTRY OF ORIGIN	YEAR INTRODUCED
ROSA ACICULARIS											
Dornroschen	dp	d	5	sv	ff	r		BS-2	Kordes	Germany	1960
ROSA ALBA											
Amelia	mp	sd	3-4	sv	fff	s	H	BS-1	Vibert	France	1823
Belle Amour	lp	d	3-4	v	fff	s	H	BS-1	found by Lindsay	France	ca. 1940
Blanche de Belgique	w	d	3-4	v	fff	s	H	BS-1	Vibert	France	1817
Blush Hip	lp	d	3-4	v	fff	s		BS-1	unknown	UK	1840
Celestial (*Celeste*)	lp	d	3-4	v	fff	s	H	BS-0	unknown	unknown	ca. 1848
Chloris (*Rosée du Matin*)	lp	d	3-4	v	ffff	s	H	BS-0	Descemet	Nether-lands	ca. 1848
Félicité Parmentier	lp	vd	3-4	sv	fff	s	H	BS-1	Parmen-tier	France	1834
Jeanne d'Arc	w	d	3-4	v	fff	s	H	BS-1	Vibert	France	1818
Maiden's Blush Great (*Rosa alba incarnata*)	lp	vd	3-4	sv	ffff	s	H	BS-1	unknown	unknown	ca. 1400
Maiden's Blush Small	lp	vd	3-4	l	ffff	s	H	BS-1	Kew Gardens	UK	1797
Maxima	w	d	3-4	v	ffff	s		BS-0	unknown	Europe	ca. 1400
Minette	lp	d	3-4	sv	fff	s	H	BS-0	unknown	France?	1819
Mme. Plantier	w	vd	3-4	v	ffff	s		BS-1	Plantier	France	1835
Pompon Blanc Parfait	w	vd	3-4	sv	fff	s		BS-1	unknown	unknown	ca. 1876
Queen of Denmark (*Königin von Dänemark*)	mp	vd	3-4	sv	fff	s	H	BS-0	Booth	Denmark	1826
Semi-Plena	w	sd	3-4	v	fff	s		BS-1	unknown	Europe	ca. 1620-30
Suaveolens	w	sd	3-4	v	fff	s		BS-0	unknown	Europe	ca. 1500
ROSA BEGGERIANA											
Mrs. John McNab	w	sd	3	sv	ff	s		BS-0	Skinner	Canada	1941
Polstjarnan	w	s	2	v	f	s		BS-0	Wasa	Finland	1937
ROSA BLANDA											
Betty Bland	dp	d	2	v	ff	s		BS-1	Skinner	Canada	1926
ROSA CENTIFOLIA											
À Long Pédoncules	lp	d	4	sv	ff	s		BS-1	Robert	France	1854
Blanche Fleur	w	d	4	sv	fff	s		BS-1	Vibert	France	1835
Blush Moss	lp	d	4	sv	fff	s		BS-1	unknown	unknown	ca. 1844
Bullata (Lettuce-leaved rose)	dp	d	4	sv	fff	s		BS-1	unknown	unknown	ca. 1500
Célina	dp	sd	4	sv	ff	s		BS-1	Hardy	France	1855

	COLOR	FORM	HARDINESS ZONE	VIGOR	FRAGRANCE	SEASON	SUITABILITY FOR HEDGING	DISEASE SUSCEPTIBILITY	BREEDER	COUNTRY OF ORIGIN	YEAR INTRODUCED
ROSA CENTIFOLIA (continued)											
Common Moss (*Old Pink Moss*), (*Communis*)	mp	d	4	sv	fff	s		BS-1	unknown	France	1696
Crested Moss (*R. centifolia cristata*), (*Chapeau de Napoléon*)	dp	d	4	sv	fff	s		BS-1	Vibert	France	1826
Crimson Moss	dr	d	4	sv	ff	s		BS-1	Lee	UK	ca. 1846
Fantin-Latour	mp	vd	4	sv	ffff	s		BS-1	Bunyard	UK	1945
Henri Martin	mr	d	4	sv	fff	s		BS-1	Laffay	France	1863
Hunslett Moss	dp	d	4	l	fff	s		BS-1	Brooke	UK	1984
Jeanne de Monfort	mp	d	4	sv	fff	s		BS-1	Robert	France	1851
La Noblesse	lp	vd	4	sv	fff	s		BS-1	unknown	unknown	1856
Marie de Blois	mp	d	4	sv	fff	c		BS-1	Robert	France	1852
Mme. Hardy	w	vd	4	sv	ffff	s		BS-1	Hardy	France	1831
Mme. William Paul	pb	d	4	l	ff	r		BS-2	Paul	UK	1869
Nuits de Young (*Old Black Moss*)	rb	d	4	sv	ff	s	H	BS-2	Laffay	France	1845
Paul Ricault	dp	vd	4	sv	fff	s		BS-1	Portemer	France	1845
Quatre Saisons Blanc Mousseux (*Perpetual White Moss*)	w	d	4	sv	ff	s		BS-1	Laffay	France	ca. 1848
Rose de Meaux	mp	vd	4	l	fff	s		BS-2	Sweet	UK	ca. 1789
Souvenir de Pierre Vibert	pb	d	4	sv	ff	r		BS-1	Morseau-Robert	France	1867
Spong	mp	d	4	sv	ff	s	H	BS-1	Spong	France	1805
Striped Moss	p/w	d	4	l	ff	s		BS-2	Verdier	France	1888
The Bishop	m	vd	4	sv	ff	s		BS-1	unknown	unknown	unknown
Tour de Malakoff (*Black Jack*)	mb	d	4	v	ff	s		BS-1	Soupert & Notting	Luxem.	1856
Violacée	mb	d	4	sv	ff	s		BS-1	Soupert & Notting	Luxem.	1876

COLOR
w = white or nearly white
p/w = pink and white
pb = pink blend
p/y = pink and yellow
lp = light pink
mp = medium pink
dp = deep pink
mr = medium red
dr = deep red
rb = red blend
m = mauve
mb = mauve blend
l = lavender
ly = light yellow
my = medium yellow
dy = deep yellow
yo = yellow-orange
o = orange
or = orange-red
c/s = coppery salmon

FORM
s = single
s+ = slightly more than single
sd = semidouble
d = double
vd = very double or quartered

HARDINESS ZONE
See zone maps on page 178–79.

VIGOR
gc = ground cover
l = low
sv = semivigorous
v = vigorous
cl = climber

FRAGRANCE
f = little or no fragrance
ff = lightly fragrant
fff = fragrant
ffff = exceptionally fragrant

SEASON
sp = spring
s = summer
r = repeating
c = continuous bloomer

SUITABILITY FOR HEDGING
H = suitable

DISEASE SUSCEPTIBILITY
Mildew:
M = particularly susceptible to mildew

Rust:
R = particularly susceptible to rust

Blackspot:
BS-0 = immune or so little as to be insignificant
BS-1 = noticeable but generally affecting fewer than 25 percent of leaves

BS-2 = affecting at least 50 percent of leaves, some defoliation without protection
BS-3 = affecting most leaves, heavy defoliation without protection

Note: Although roses are subject to several diseases, by far the most important disease of hardy cultivars is blackspot. Those in drier climates may not have problems with blackspot, but in more humid areas blackspot can seriously affect many roses. These designations are based on the incidence of blackspot at a moderately humid site. Although you may find the incidence of blackspot either more or less severe than indicated by these ratings, they at least will offer a relative scale of blackspot susceptibility.

THE CULTIVARS	COLOR	FORM	HARDINESS ZONE	VIGOR	FRAGRANCE	SEASON	SUITABILITY FOR HEDGING	DISEASE SUSCEPTIBILITY	BREEDER	COUNTRY OF ORIGIN	YEAR INTRODUCED
ROSA CENTIFOLIA (continued)											
White Bath	w	d	4	sv	fff	s		BS-1	Salter	UK	1817
William Lobb (*Old Velvet Moss*)	mb	d	4	v	fff	s		BS-1	Laffay	France	1855
ROSA CINNAMOMEA											
Plena (*Cinnamon*)	mp	d	3	sv	fff	s	H	BS-0	unknown	unknown	ca. 1583
ROSA EGLANTERIA											
Amy Robsart	dp	s	4	v	ff	s	H	BS-3	Penzance	UK	1894
Goldbusch	my	sd	4	v	fff	s	H	BS-1	Kordes	Germany	1954
Greenmantle	r	s	4	v	ff	s	H	BS-3	Penzance	UK	1894
Hebe's Lip (*Rubrotincta*), (*Reine Blanche*)	w	s	4	sv	ff	s	H	BS-2	Paul	UK	1912
Herbstfeuer (*Autumn Fire*)	dr	sd	4	v	f	r	H	BS-1	Kordes	Germany	1961
Julia Mannering	lp	s	4	v	ff	s	H	BS-2	Penzance	UK	1895
La Belle Distinguée (*Scarlet Sweetbriar*), (*La Petite Duchesse*)	dr	d	4	sv	f	s	H	BS-2	unknown	unknown	unknown
Lady Penzance	p/y	s	4	v	ff	s	H	BS-3	Penzance	UK	1894
Lord Pensance	p/y	s	4	v	ff	s	H	BS-3	Penzance	UK	1890
Manning's Blush	w	d	4	sv	ff	s	H	BS-2	unknown	unknown	ca. 1800
Meg Merrilees	dr	sd	4	v	ff	s	H	BS-3	Penzance	UK	ca. 1894
ROSA FOETIDA											
Austrian Copper	or	s	3-4	sv	f	s		BS-3	unknown	Asia	ca. 1500
Lawrence Johnston	dy	sd	5	cl	ff	r		BS-3	Pernet-Ducher	France	1923
Persian Yellow	dy	d	3-4	sv	ff	s		BS-3	unknown	S.W. Asia	1835
Soleil d'Or	yo	d	4-5	sv	fff	r		BS-3	Pernet-Ducher	France	1900
ROSA GALLICA											
Agatha (*Agathe*)	dp	sd	3-4	sv	ff	s		BS-1	unknown	Europe	unknown
Alain Blanchard	rb	sd	4	sv	fff	s		BS-1	Vibert	France	1839
Alika (*Gallica grandiflora*)	mr	sd	3-4	v	fff	s		BS-1	Hanson	unknown	1906
Anaïs Ségalas	rb	d	4	l	fff	s		BS-1	Vibert	France	1837
Antonia d'Ormois	lp	d	4	sv	ff	s		BS-1	Roseraie de l'Hay	France	unknown
Apothecary's Rose (*Rosa gallica officinalis*)	dp	sd	4	sv	fff	s		BS-1	unknown	unknown	ca. 1600

THE CULTIVARS	COLOR	FORM	HARDINESS ZONE	VIGOR	FRAGRANCE	SEASON	SUITABILITY FOR HEDGING	DISEASE SUSCEPTIBILITY	BREEDER	COUNTRY OF ORIGIN	YEAR INTRODUCED
ROSA GALLICA (continued)											
Assemblage des Beautés (*Rouge Eblouissante*)	dr	vd	4	sv	ff	s		BS-1	unknown	France	ca. 1823
Belle de Crécy	mb	d	4	sv	fff	s		BS-1	unknown	unknown	ca. 1850
Belle Isis	lp	vd	4	l	fff	s		BS-1	Parmentier	Belgium	1845
Camaieux	p/w	vd	4	l	ff	s		BS-1	Vibert	France	1830
Cardinal de Richelieu	mb	vd	3-4	l	ffff	s		BS-1	Parmentier	Belgium	1840
Charles de Mills	rb	vd	3	sv	ffff	s		BS-1	unknown	Netherlands	ca. 1700
Complicata	mp	s	4-5	v	ff	s		BS-1	unknown	unknown	old
Comte de Nanteuil	mb	d	4	sv	ff	s		BS-1	Roeser	France	1834
Comtesse de Lacépède	w	vd	4	sv	ff	s		BS-1	unknown	France	1840
Conditorum	dr	sd	4	sv	fff	s		BS-1	unknown	France	old
Cosimo Ridolfi	mb	vd	4	l	ff	s		BS-1	Vibert	France	1842
Cramoisi Picoté	rb	vd	4	l	f	s		BS-1	Vibert	France	1834
D'Agnesseau	dr	vd	4	sv	ff	s		BS-1	Vibert	France	1823
Duc de Fitzjames	mb	vd	4	sv	ff	s		BS-1	unknown	unknown	ca. 1885
Duc de Guiche	rb	d	4	sv	fff	s		BS-1	Prévost	France	1835
Duchesse d'Angolême (*Duc d'Angoulême*)	lp	vd	4	sv	fff	s		BS-1	Vibert	France	ca. 1835
Duchesse de Buccleugh	rb	vd	4	v	ff	s		BS-1	Robert	France	1860
Duchesse de Montebello	lp	vd	4	sv	fff	s		BS-1	Laffay	France	1829
George Vibert	pb	d	4	sv	ff	s		BS-1	Robert	France	1853
Gloire De France	lp	vd	4	l	ff	s		BS-2	unknown	unknown	ca. 1819
Gros Provins Panaché	mb	d	4	sv	fff	s		BS-1	unknown	unknown	unknown
Henri Fouquier	mp	vd	4	l	fff	s		BS-1	unknown	unknown	1854
Hippolyte	mb	vd	4	v	ff	s		BS-1	unknown	unknown	ca. 1820
Ipsilanté	pb	v	4	sv	fff	s		BS-1	unknown	unknown	1821

COLOR
w = white or nearly white
p/w = pink and white
pb = pink blend
p/y = pink and yellow
lp = light pink
mp = medium pink
dp = deep pink
mr = medium red
dr = deep red
rb = red blend
m   = mauve
mb = mauve blend
l   = lavender
ly = light yellow
my = medium yellow
dy = deep yellow
yo = yellow-orange
o   = orange
or = orange-red
c/s = coppery salmon

FORM
s   = single
s+ = slightly more than single
sd = semidouble
d   = double
vd = very double or quartered

HARDINESS ZONE
See zone maps on page 178–79.

VIGOR
gc = ground cover
l   = low
sv = semivigorous
v   = vigorous
cl = climber

FRAGRANCE
f   = little or no fragrance
ff   = lightly fragrant
fff = fragrant
ffff = exceptionally fragrant

SEASON
sp = spring
s   = summer
r   = repeating
c   = continuous bloomer

SUITABILITY FOR HEDGING
H = suitable

DISEASE SUSCEPTIBILITY
Mildew:
M = particularly susceptible to mildew

Rust:
R = particularly susceptible to rust

Blackspot:
BS-0 = immune or so little as to be insignificant
BS-1 = noticeable but generally affecting fewer than 25 percent of leaves

BS-2 = affecting at least 50 percent of leaves, some defoliation without protection
BS-3 = affecting most leaves, heavy defoliation without protection

Note: Although roses are subject to several diseases, by far the most important disease of hardy cultivars is blackspot. Those in drier climates may not have problems with blackspot, but in more humid areas blackspot can seriously affect many roses. These designations are based on the incidence of blackspot at a moderately humid site. Although you may find the incidence of blackspot either more or less severe than indicated by these ratings, they at least will offer a relative scale of blackspot susceptibility.

THE CULTIVARS	COLOR	FORM	HARDINESS ZONE	VIGOR	FRAGRANCE	SEASON	SUITABILITY FOR HEDGING	DISEASE SUSCEPTIBILITY	BREEDER	COUNTRY OF ORIGIN	YEAR INTRODUCED
ROSA GALLICA (continued)											
James Mason	dr	sd	4	sv	ff	s		BS-1	Beales	UK	1982
Jenny Duval	mb	sd	4	sv	fff	s		BS-1, M	unknown	unknown	ca. 1750
La Belle Sutane (*Violacea*)	mb	sd	4	v	ff	s		BS-1	unknown	unknown	1795
La Plus Belle des Ponctuées	pb	vd	4	v	ff	s		BS-1	unknown	unknown	unknown
Nestor	pb	d	4	sv	ff	s		BS-1	unknown	unknown	ca. 1846
Oeillet Flamand	pb	vd	4	sv	ff	s		BS-1	Vibert	France	1845
Oeillet Parfait	w	vd	4	v	ff	s		BS-0	Foulard	France	1841
Ombrée Parfaite	pb	vd	4	l	ff	s		BS-1	Vibert	France	1823
Perle de Panachées	p/w	d	4	v	ff	s		BS-1	Vibert	France	1845
Président de Sèze (*Mme. Hébert*)	pb	vd	4	sv	ff	s		BS-1	unknown	unknown	ca. 1836
Rosa Mundi (*R. gallica versicolor*)	p/w	d	3	sv	fff	s		BS-1	unknown	Europe	ca. 1580
Rose du Maître d'Ecole	dp	v	4	l	ff	s		BS-1	Miellez	France	1840
Sissinghurst Castle (*Rose des Maures*)	dr	vd	4	l	ff	s		BS-1	unknown	unknown	old
Surpasse Tout	rb	vd	4	sv	ff	s		BS-1	unknown	unknown	ca. 1832
Tricolore (*Reine Marguerite*)	dp	vd	4	sv	ff	s		BS-1	Lahaye Père	France	1827
Tricolore de Flandre	pb	vd	4	sv	ff	s		BS-1	Van Houtte	Belgium	1846
Tuscany (*Old Velvet Rose*)	rb	d	4	sv	ffff	s		BS-1	unknown	Italy?	ca. 1500
Tuscany Superb	rb	d	4	sv	fff	s		BS-2	Paul	UK	1848
ROSA GLAUCA											
Carmenetta	mp	s	2	v	f	s		BS-0	Preston	Canada	1923
ROSA HELENAE											
Patricia Macoun	w	d	4	v	ff	s		BS-2	Preston	Canada	1945
ROSA MOYESII											
Eddie's Crimson	dr	d	4	v	f	s		BS-1	Eddie	Canada	1956
Eddie's Jewel	mr	d	4	v	f	r		BS-1	Eddie	Canada	1962
Fred Streeter	dp	s	4	v	f	s		BS-1	Jackman	UK	1951
Geranium	or	s	3-4	v	f	s		BS-0	Mulligan	UK	1938
Highodensis	dp	s	3-4	v	f	s		BS-0	Hillier	UK	1928
Marguerite Hilling	mp	s+	5	v	f	r		BS-1	Hillier	UK	1959
Nevada	w	s+	5	v	f	r		BS-1	Dot	Spain	1927

THE CULTIVARS

	COLOR	FORM	HARDINESS ZONE	VIGOR	FRAGRANCE	SEASON	SUITABILITY FOR HEDGING	DISEASE SUSCEPTIBILITY	BREEDER	COUNTRY OF ORIGIN	YEAR INTRODUCED
ROSA MULTIFLORA											
Ames Climber	w	s	3	cl	f	s		BS-1	Maney	USA	1932
ROSA NITIDA											
Alysham	dp	d	3	l	f	s		BS-0	Wright	Canada	1948
Defender	dp	s	2-3	sv	ff	s		BS-0	Darthuis	Netherlands	1971
Métis	mp	d	2-3	sv	ff	s	H	BS-0	Simonet	Canada	1967
ROSA POLYANTHA											
The Fairy	lp	d	4-5	l	f	c		BS-1	Bentall	UK	1932
ROSA RUBRIFOLIA (GLAUCA)											
Carmenetta	mp	s	2	v	f	s		BS-0	Preston	Canada	1923
ROSA RUGOSA											
Agnes	my	d	3	sv	fff	r	H	BS-0	Saunders	Canada	1922
Amelie Gravereaux	rb	d	3	v	fff	r	H	BS-0	Gravereaux	France	1903
Belle Poitvine	mp	sd	4	sv	ff	r	H	BS-0	Bruant	France	1984
Blanc Double de Coubert	w	sd	2-3	v	ffff	r	H	BS-0	Cochet-Cochet	France	1892
Carmen	dr	s	4	sv	ff	r	H	BS-1	Lambert	Germany	1907
Charles Albanel	m	sd	2-3	gc	fff	c		BS-0	Svejda	Canada	1982
Conrad Ferdinand Meyer	mp	d	4-5	v	fff	r	H	BS-2, R	Müller	Germany	1899
Culverbrae	dr	vd	4	sv	ff	r	H	BS-0	Gobbee	UK	1973
Dart's Dash	m	sd	2-3	sv	fff	c	H	BS-0, M	Darthuis Nursery	Netherlands	ca. 1980
David Thompson	dp	d	2-3	sv	fff	c	H	BS-0	Svejda	Canada	1979

COLOR
w = white or nearly white
p/w = pink and white
pb = pink blend
p/y = pink and yellow
lp = light pink
mp = medium pink
dp = deep pink
mr = medium red
dr = deep red
rb = red blend
m = mauve
mb = mauve blend
l = lavender
ly = light yellow
my = medium yellow
dy = deep yellow
yo = yellow-orange
o = orange
or = orange-red
c/s = coppery salmon

FORM
s = single
s+ = slightly more than single
sd = semidouble
d = double
vd = very double or quartered

HARDINESS ZONE
See zone maps on page 178-79.

VIGOR
gc = ground cover
l = low
sv = semivigorous
v = vigorous
cl = climber

FRAGRANCE
f = little or no fragrance
ff = lightly fragrant
fff = fragrant
ffff = exceptionally fragrant

SEASON
sp = spring
s = summer
r = repeating
c = continuous bloomer

SUITABILITY FOR HEDGING
H = suitable

DISEASE SUSCEPTIBILITY
Mildew:
M = particularly susceptible to mildew

Rust:
R = particularly susceptible to rust

Blackspot:
BS-0 = immune or so little as to be insignificant
BS-1 = noticeable but generally affecting fewer than 25 percent of leaves

BS-2 = affecting at least 50 percent of leaves, some defoliation without protection
BS-3 = affecting most leaves, heavy defoliation without protection

Note: Although roses are subject to several diseases, by far the most important disease of hardy cultivars is blackspot. Those in drier climates may not have problems with blackspot, but in more humid areas blackspot can seriously affect many roses. These designations are based on the incidence of blackspot at a moderately humid site. Although you may find the incidence of blackspot either more or less severe than indicated by these ratings, they at least will offer a relative scale of blackspot susceptibility.

THE CULTIVARS	COLOR	FORM	HARDINESS ZONE	VIGOR	FRAGRANCE	SEASON	SUITABILITY FOR HEDGING	DISEASE SUSCEPTIBILITY	BREEDER	COUNTRY OF ORIGIN	YEAR INTRODUCED
ROSA RUGOSA (continued)											
Delicata	mp	sd	3	sv	fff	r	H	BS-0	Cooling	UK	1898
Dr. Eckener	p/y	sd	5	v	fff	r		BS-1	Berger	Germany	1930
Dwarf Pavement	mp	sd	2-3	sv	fff	r	H	BS-0	Uhl	Germany	unknown
Fimbriata	lp	sd	4	sv	f	r	H	BS-0	Morlet	France	1891
F.J. Grootendorst	mr	d	3-4	v	f	c		BS-1	De Goey or Skinner	Nether-lands or Canada	1918 or 1908
Foxi Pavement	dp	sd	2-3	sv	fff	r	H	BS-0	Uhl	Germany	ca. 1987
Frü Dagmar Hastrup (*Frü Dagmar Hartopp*)	mp	s	2-3	l	fff	c		BS-0	Hastrup	Denmark	1914
George Will	dp	d	2-3	sv	fff	r		BS-1	Skinner	Canada	1939
Grootendorst Supreme	dr	d	3-4	v	f	c	H	BS-1	Grooten-dorst	Nether-lands	1936
Hansa	m	d	2	v	fff	r	H	BS-0	Schaum & Van Tol	Nether-lands	1905
Hansaland	dr	sd	3	sv	f	r		BS-1	Kordes	Germany	1993
Henry Hudson	w	d	2-3	l	fff	c		BS-0	Svejda	Canada	1979
Hunter	dr	d	4	sv	fff	c		BS-1	Mattock	UK	1961
Jens Munk	mp	sd	2-3	sv	fff	c	H	BS-0	Svejda	Canada	1979
Lac La Nonne	pb	d	2	v	fff	s		BS-0	Bugnet	Canada	ca. 1950
Lac Majeau	w	d	2	v	fff	s	H	BS-0	Bugnet	Canada	ca. 1981
Lady Curzon	lp	s	4	sv	fff	r		BS-1	Turner	UK	1901
Linda Campbell	dr	sd	3-4	sv	ff	c	H	BS-2	Moore	USA	1991
Louise Bugnet	w	d	2	v	fff	r	H	BS-0	Bugnet	Canada	ca. 1960
Magnifica	mr	sd	3	sv	fff	r	H	BS-0	Van Fleet	USA	1905
Marie Bugnet	w	d	2-3	sv	fff	r	H	BS-0	Bugnet	Canada	1963
Martin Frobisher	lp	d	3	v	fff	c	H	BS-0	Svejda	Canada	1968
Mary Manners	w	sd	4	v	fff	c	H	BS-1	Leicester Rose Co.	England	1970
Max Graf	dp	s	4	gc	ff	s		BS-0	Bowditch	USA	1919
Mme. Georges Bruant	w	sd	4	sv	fff	c	H	BS-0	Bruant	France	1887
Mrs. Anthony Waterer	dr	d	3	sv	f	c	H	BS-2	Waterer	UK	1898
Moje Hammarberg	m	d	3	v	fff	r	H	BS-0	Hammar-berg	Sweden	1931
Musician	pb	d	2	sv	f	s		BS-0	Wright	Canada	1953
Nova Zembla	w	d	5	v	fff	r	H	BS-1, R	Mees	UK	1907
Nyveldt's White	w	s	4	sv	fff	r	H	BS-1	Nyveldt	Nether-lands	1955
Parfum de l'Hay	dr	d	4	sv	ffff	c		BS-1	Graver-eaux	France	1901
Pierette Pavement	mp	sd	2-3	sv	fff	r	H	BS-0	Uhl	Germany	1987

THE CULTIVARS

	COLOR	FORM	HARDINESS ZONE	VIGOR	FRAGRANCE	SEASON	SUITABILITY FOR HEDGING	DISEASE SUSCEPTIBILITY	BREEDER	COUNTRY OF ORIGIN	YEAR INTRODUCED
ROSA RUGOSA (continued)											
Pink Grootendorst	mp	d	3-4	sv	f	c	H	BS-1	Grooten-dorst	Nether-lands	1923
Pink Pavement	mp	sd	2-3	sv	fff	r	H	BS-0	Uhl	Germany	1985
Polareis	w	sd	2	sv	ff	r	H	BS-1	Rieksta	Latvia	1988
Pristine Pavement	w	sd	2-3	sv	fff	r	H	BS-0	Baum	Germany	1990
Purple Pavement	m	sd	2-3	sv	fff	r	H	BS-0	Baum	Germany	1983
Rita Bugnet	w	d	2	sv	fff	r		BS-0	Bugnet	Canada	ca. 1960
Rosa Paulii	w	s	2-3	gc	fff	s		BS-0, M	Paul	UK	1903
Roseraie de l'Hay	dr	sd	3	v	ffff	c	H	BS-0	Cochet-Cochet	France	1901
Rugosa repens rosea (*Rosa × paulii rosea*)	lp	s	2-3	gc	fff	s		BS-0	Paul	UK	1912
Ruskin	dr	d	3-4	v	fff	r	H	BS-1	Van Fleet	USA	1928
Sarah Van Fleet	mp	sd	4	sv	fff	c	H	BS-1, R	Van Fleet	USA	1926
Scabrosa	m	s	2-3	v	fff	c	H	BS-0	Harkness	UK	1960
Scarlet Pavement	dp	sd	2-3	sv	fff	r	H	BS-0	Uhl	Germany	unknown
Schneelicht	w	s	4	v	ff	r	H	BS-1	Gesch-wind	Hungary	1894
Schneezwerg (*Snow Dwarf*)	w	sd	2-3	sv	fff	c	H	BS-0	Lambert	Germany	1912
Sir Thomas Lipton	w	d	3-4	v	fff	c	H	BS-0	Van Fleet	USA	1900
Snow Pavement (*Schneeköppe*)	w	sd	2-3	sv	ffff	r	H	BS-0	Baum	Germany	1986
Souvenir de Philemon Cochet	w	d	2-3	v	ffff	c	H	BS-0	Cochet	France	1899
Thérèse Bugnet	mp	d	2	v	ffff	r	H	BS-0, M	Bugnet	Canada	1950
Topaz Jewel	my	sd	5	sv	ff	r		BS-2	Moore	USA	1987
Vanguard	c/s	sd	5	v	fff	r	H	BS-1	Stevens	USA	1932

COLOR
w = white or nearly white
p/w = pink and white
pb = pink blend
p/y = pink and yellow
lp = light pink
mp = medium pink
dp = deep pink
mr = medium red
dr = deep red
rb = red blend
m = mauve
mb = mauve blend
l = lavender
ly = light yellow
my = medium yellow
dy = deep yellow
yo = yellow-orange
o = orange
or = orange-red
c/s = coppery salmon

FORM
s = single
s+ = slightly more than single
sd = semidouble
d = double
vd = very double or quartered

HARDINESS ZONE
See zone maps on page 178–79.

VIGOR
gc = ground cover
l = low
sv = semivigorous
v = vigorous
cl = climber

FRAGRANCE
f = little or no fragrance
ff = lightly fragrant
fff = fragrant
ffff = exceptionally fragrant

SEASON
sp = spring
s = summer
r = repeating
c = continuous bloomer

SUITABILITY FOR HEDGING
H = suitable

DISEASE SUSCEPTIBILITY
Mildew:
M = particularly susceptible to mildew

Rust:
R = particularly susceptible to rust

Blackspot:
BS-0 = immune or so little as to be insignificant
BS-1 = noticeable but generally affecting fewer than 25 percent of leaves

BS-2 = affecting at least 50 percent of leaves, some defoliation without protection
BS-3 = affecting most leaves, heavy defoliation without protection

Note: Although roses are subject to several diseases, by far the most important disease of hardy cultivars is blackspot. Those in drier climates may not have problems with blackspot, but in more humid areas blackspot can seriously affect many roses. These designations are based on the incidence of blackspot at a moderately humid site. Although you may find the incidence of blackspot either more or less severe than indicated by these ratings, they at least will offer a relative scale of blackspot susceptibility.

THE CULTIVARS	COLOR	FORM	HARDINESS ZONE	VIGOR	FRAGRANCE	SEASON	SUITABILITY FOR HEDGING	DISEASE SUSCEPTIBILITY	BREEDER	COUNTRY OF ORIGIN	YEAR INTRODUCED
ROSA RUGOSA (continued)											
Wasagaming	mp	d	2-3	sv	fff	s		BS-1	Skinner	Canada	1938
White Grootendorst	w	d	3-4	sv	f	c		BS-1	Eddie	UK	1962
White Pavement	w	sd	2-3	sv	fff	r	H	BS-0	Uhl	Germany	unknown
Will Alderman	mp	d	2-3	sv	ff	c		BS-1	Skinner	Canada	1949
ROSA SETIGERA											
American Pillar	dp	s	5	cl	f	s		BS-0	Van Fleet	USA	1902
Balimore Belle	lp	d	5	cl	f	s		BS-1	Feast	USA	1843
ROSA SPINOSISSIMA (*ROSA PIMPINELLIFOLIA*)											
Aïcha	my	s+	3	cl	fff	sp		BS-1	Petersen	Denmark	1966
Altaica	w	s	3	sv	f	sp	H	BS-0	Species	Asia	ca. 1818
Dr. Merkeley	mp	d	2	l	fff	s		BS-1	unknown	Russia?	ca. 1924
Doorenbos selection	rb	s	3	l	ff	r		BS-0	Dooren-bos?	Germa-ny?	unknown
Double pink (*Burnet double pink*)	mp	d	3	sv	ffff	sp		BS-0	unknown	UK	ca. 1800s
Double white (*Burnet double white*)	w	d	3	sv	ffff	sp		BS-0	unknown	UK	ca. 1800s
Double yellow (*Old Yellow Scotch*)	my	d	3	sv	ff	sp		BS-1	unknown	UK	ca. 1800s
Frühlingsanfang	w	s	4-5	v	fff	sp	H	BS-1	Kordes	Germany	1950
Frühlingsduft	ab	sd	4-5	v	fff	sp	H	BS-1	Kordes	Germany	1949
Frühlingsgold	my	s+	4-5	v	ff	sp	H	BS-2	Kordes	Germany	1937
Frühlingsmorgen	dp	s	4-5	v	fff	r	H	BS-1	Kordes	Germany	1942
Frühlingschnee	w	sd	4-5	v	ff	sp	H	BS-1	Kordes	Germany	1954
Frühlingstag	dy	sd	4-5	v	fff	sp	H	BS-1	Kordes	Germany	1949
Gloire de Edzell (*Glory of Edzell*)	mp	s	4	v	ff	sp	H	BS-1	unknown	unknown	unknown
Harison's Salmon	c/s	s	3	sv	ff	sp	H	BS-0	Hamblin	USA	1929
Harison's Yellow (*Yellow Rose of Texas*), (*R. × Harisonii*)	my	sd	3	sv	ff	sp	H	BS-1	Harison	USA	1825
Hazeldean	my	sd	2-3	sv	fff	sp	H	BS-1	Wright	Canada	1948
Kakwa	lp	d	2	sv	ffff	sp	H	BS-0	Wallace	Canada	1973
Karl Förster	w	sd	4-5	sv	fff	r		BS-0	Kordes	Germany	1953
Maigold	yo	sd	5	v	fff	s		BS-1	Kordes	Germany	1953
Mary Queen of Scots	mp	s	3	l	ff	sp		BS-1	unknown	UK?	unknown
Mrs. Colville	rb	s	3	sv	ff	sp		BS-1	unknown	UK?	unknown
Petite Pink Scotch	mp	s	3	gc	ff	sp		BS-1	unknown	UK?	ca. 1750
Prairie Peace	p/y	sd	2	v	ff	s		BS-1	Erskine	Canada	ca. 1975

THE CULTIVARS	COLOR	FORM	HARDINESS ZONE	VIGOR	FRAGRANCE	SEASON	SUITABILITY FOR HEDGING	DISEASE SUSCEPTIBILITY	BREEDER	COUNTRY OF ORIGIN	YEAR INTRODUCED
ROSA SPINOSISSIMA (*ROSA PIMPINELLIFOLIA*) (continued)											
Single Cherry	mr	s	3	l	ff	sp		BS-1	unknown	UK?	unknown
Stanwell Perpetual	lp	d	3	sv	ffff	c	H	BS-0	Lee	UK	1838
Suzanne	lp	vd	3	sv	f	c		BS-1	Skinner	Canada	1949
William III	mb	sd	3	l	fff	s		BS-1	unknown	UK?	unknown
Williams' Double	y	d	2	sv	ff	s		BS-2	Williams	UK	1820
ROSA SUFFULTA											
Assiniboine	dp	d	3	sv	ff	s		BS-1	Marshall	Canada	1962
Cuthbert Grant	dr	d	3-4	sv	f	c		BS-1	Marshall	Canada	1967
ROSA XANTHINA											
Canary Bird	dy	s	4-5	sv	f	sp		BS-1	unknown	unknown	1907
MISCELLANEOUS SHRUBS											
Adelaide Hoodless	dr	sd	4	l	f	r		BS-2	Marshall	Canada	1973
Alexander Mackenzie	mr	d	3-4	v	fff	c	H	BS-0	Svejda	Canada	1985
Aurora Borealis	mp	d	3	sv	f	c		BS-1	Conev-Sandhu	Canada	2021
Bassino	dr	s	4	gc	f	c		BS-1	Kordes	Germany	1988
Birdie Blye	mp	d	4-5	sv	f	r	H	BS-1	Van Fleet	USA	1904
Bonica '82 (Bonica)	lp	d	5	l	f	c	H	BS-1	Meilland	France	1985
Campfire	p/y	sd	3	l	f	c		BS-1	Dyck	Canada	2012
Canada Blooms	mp	vd	4	l	ffff	c		BS-1	Richer	Canada	2014
Canadian Shield	dr	d	3	v	f	c		BS-0	Dyck	Canada	2017
Captain Samuel Holland	lr	sd	3-4	v	f	r		BS-0	Svejda	Canada	1990
Carefree Beauty (*Bucbi*), (*Audace*)	mp	sd	4	sv	fff	r		BS-1	Buck	USA	ca. 1976

COLOR

w = white or nearly white
p/w = pink and white
pb = pink blend
p/y = pink and yellow
lp = light pink
mp = medium pink
dp = deep pink
mr = medium red
dr = deep red
rb = red blend
m = mauve
mb = mauve blend
l = lavender
ly = light yellow
my = medium yellow
dy = deep yellow
yo = yellow-orange
o = orange
or = orange-red
c/s = coppery salmon

FORM

s = single
s+ = slightly more than single
sd = semidouble
d = double
vd = very double or quartered

HARDINESS ZONE

See zone maps on page 178–79.

VIGOR

gc = ground cover
l = low
sv = semivigorous
v = vigorous
cl = climber

FRAGRANCE

f = little or no fragrance
ff = lightly fragrant
fff = fragrant
ffff = exceptionally fragrant

SEASON

sp = spring
s = summer
r = repeating
c = continuous bloomer

SUITABILITY FOR HEDGING

H = suitable

DISEASE SUSCEPTIBILITY

Mildew:
M = particularly susceptible to mildew

Rust:
R = particularly susceptible to rust

Blackspot:
BS-0 = immune or so little as to be insignificant
BS-1 = noticeable but generally affecting fewer than 25 percent of leaves

BS-2 = affecting at least 50 percent of leaves, some defoliation without protection
BS-3 = affecting most leaves, heavy defoliation without protection

Note: Although roses are subject to several diseases, by far the most important disease of hardy cultivars is blackspot. Those in drier climates may not have problems with blackspot, but in more humid areas blackspot can seriously affect many roses. These designations are based on the incidence of blackspot at a moderately humid site. Although you may find the incidence of blackspot either more or less severe than indicated by these ratings, they at least will offer a relative scale of blackspot susceptibility.

THE CULTIVARS	COLOR	FORM	HARDINESS ZONE	VIGOR	FRAGRANCE	SEASON	SUITABILITY FOR HEDGING	DISEASE SUSCEPTIBILITY	BREEDER	COUNTRY OF ORIGIN	YEAR INTRODUCED
MISCELLANEOUS SHRUBS (continued)											
Champlain	dr	sd	4	l	ff	c		BS-0	Svejda	Canada	1982
Chinook Sunrise	c/s	sd	3	sv	f	c		BS-1	Conev-Sandhu	Canada	2019
Constance Spry (*Constanze Spry*)	mp	d	4	v	fff	s		BS-0	Austin	UK	1961
Cuthbert Grant	dr	d	4	sv	ff	r		BS-2	Agr. Canada	Canada	1967
De Montarville	lr	sd	4	l	f	r		BS-0	Agr. Canada	Canada	1997
Dortmund	dr	s	5	cl	f	r		BS-1	Kordes	Germany	1955
Dr. Merkeley	mp	d	2-3	l	fff	s	H	BS-0	unknown	Siberia int	1924
Emily Carr	r	sd	3	sv	f	c		BS-1	Collicutt	Canada	2007
Felix Leclerc	dp	sd	3	cl	ff	r		BS-0	Svejda	Canada	2007
Flamingo	mp	sd	5	v	ff	r		BS-1	Howard	USA	1956
Frontenac	mp	sd	3-4	l	ff	c	H	BS-0	Svejda	Canada	1993
George Vancouver	lr	sd	3	sv	f	r	H	BS-0	Svejda	Canada	1994
Golden Wings	my	s+	5	sv	ff	c		BS-2	Shepherd	USA	1956
Henry Kelsey	dr	sd	4	cl	ff	c		BS-1	Svejda	Canada	1986
Hope for Humanity	dr	d	3-4	l	f	r		BS-1	Agr. Canada	Canada	1995
John Cabot	mr	d	3	cl	ff	c		BS-0	Svejda	Canada	1978
John Davis	mp	d	3	v	ff	c		BS-0	Svejda	Canada	1986
John Franklin	mr	sd	4-5	l	f	c		BS-2	Svejda	Canada	1980
J.H. Kern	m	vd	4	l	ff	c		BS-2	Kern?	USA?	unknown
J.P. Connell	my	d	3-4	sv	fff	r		BS-2	Svejda	Canada	1987
Lambert Closse	lp	d	4	l	ff	r		BS-1	Agr. Canada	Canada	1995
Lavender Bouquet	l	d	4	v	f	r		BS-0	MacPhail	Canada	2019
Leverkusen	my	sd	4-5	cl	ff	s	H	BS-0	Kordes	Germany	1954
Louis Jolliet	dp	d	3	v	f	c	H	BS-0	Agr. Canada	Canada	1990
Lucy Irene	lp	sd	2	v	ff	r	H	BS-1	Nichol-son	Canada	2012
Marie Bugnet	w	sd	2-3	v	fff	r	H	BS-1	Bugnet	Canada	1963
Marie-Victorin	p/y	d	3-4	sv	fff	r		BS-1	Svejda	Canada	1998
Morden 6910	dr	s	3	cl	f	s	H	BS-1	Harp	Canada	1969
Morden Amorette	mr	d	3-4	l	f	c		BS-2	Marshall	Canada	1977
Morden Blush	w/lp	d	3	l	ff	c		BS-2	Marshall	Canada	1976
Morden Cardinette	mr	d	3-4	l	f	c		BS-2	Marshall	Canada	1980
Morden Centennial	mp	d	3	sv	ff	r		BS-1	Marshall	Canada	1980
Morden Fireglow	or	sd	3	l	f	c		BS-2	Collicutt-Marshall	Canada	1989
Morden Ruby	dp	d	3	l	f	c		BS-2	Marshall	Canada	1977

	COLOR	FORM	HARDINESS ZONE	VIGOR	FRAGRANCE	SEASON	SUITABILITY FOR HEDGING	DISEASE SUSCEPTIBILITY	BREEDER	COUNTRY OF ORIGIN	YEAR INTRODUCED
MISCELLANEOUS SHRUBS (continued)											
Morden Snow Beauty	w	s+	3-4	l	ff	r		BS-1	Collicutt	Canada	2001
Morden Sunrise	y	s+	3-4	l	f	r		BS-1	Agr. Canada	Canada	1999
Mrs. John McNabb	w	vd	3	sv	ff	r	H	BS-1	Skinner	Canada	1942
Nearly Wild	mp	s	3-4	l	f	c		BS-1	Brownell	USA	1941
Nicholas	dr	sd	3	l	f	r		BS-1	Svejda	Canada	1996
Oscar Peterson	w	sd	3	v	f	c	H	BS-1	Dyck	Canada	2016
Parkdirector Riggers	dr	s+	5	v	f	c		BS-1	Kordes	Germany	1957
Polstjärnan (*Polestar*), (*The Polar Star*), (*The Wasa Star*), (*The White Star of Finland*), (*Wasatjernan*)	w	s	3	cl	f	s		BS-0	Wasat-Jarnan	Finland	1937
Prairie Dawn	mp	d	3	v	f	s		BS-1	Agr. Canada	Canada	1959
Prairie Joy	mp	d	3	l	f	r	H	BS-2	Collicutt-Marshall	Canada	1990
Quadra	dr	vd	3	v	f	r		BS-0	Svejda	Canada	1994
Ramblin' Red	dr	d	4	v	fff	r		BS-1	Radler	USA	2002
Raubritter	p	d	4	sv	fff	s		BS-1	Kordes	Germany	1936
Rheinaupark	dr	sd	5	sv	f	c		BS-2	Kordes	Germany	1983
Robusta	dr	s	4-5	v	ff	c		BS-1	Kordes	Germany	1987
Rote Max Graf (*Red Max Graf*), (*Kormax*), (*Kordes' rose*)	dr	s	5	gc	f	s		BS-0	Kordes	Germany	1980
Royal Edward	mp	s+	4	l	f	r		BS-0	Agr. Canada	Canada	1995
Scharlachglut (*Scarlet Glow*), (*Scarlet Fire*)	dr	s	3-4	v	ff	s		BS-1	Kordes	Germany	1952
Shropshire Lass	lp	s+	5	v	ff	s		BS-1	Austin	UK	1968
Simon Fraser	mp	s+	3	l	f	c	H	BS-0	Svejda	Canada	1992

COLOR
w = white or nearly white
p/w = pink and white
pb = pink blend
p/y = pink and yellow
lp = light pink
mp = medium pink
dp = deep pink
mr = medium red
dr = deep red
rb = red blend
m = mauve
mb = mauve blend
l = lavender
ly = light yellow
my = medium yellow
dy = deep yellow
yo = yellow-orange
o = orange
or = orange-red
c/s = coppery salmon

FORM
s = single
s+ = slightly more than single
sd = semidouble
d = double
vd = very double or quartered

HARDINESS ZONE
See zone maps on page 178–79.

VIGOR
gc = ground cover
l = low
sv = semivigorous
v = vigorous
cl = climber

FRAGRANCE
f = little or no fragrance
ff = lightly fragrant
fff = fragrant
ffff = exceptionally fragrant

SEASON
sp = spring
s = summer
r = repeating
c = continuous bloomer

SUITABILITY FOR HEDGING
H = suitable

DISEASE SUSCEPTIBILITY
Mildew:
M = particularly susceptible to mildew

Rust:
R = particularly susceptible to rust

Blackspot:
BS-0 = immune or so little as to be insignificant
BS-1 = noticeable but generally affecting fewer than 25 percent of leaves

BS-2 = affecting at least 50 percent of leaves, some defoliation without protection
BS-3 = affecting most leaves, heavy defoliation without protection

Note: Although roses are subject to several diseases, by far the most important disease of hardy cultivars is blackspot. Those in drier climates may not have problems with blackspot, but in more humid areas blackspot can seriously affect many roses. These designations are based on the incidence of blackspot at a moderately humid site. Although you may find the incidence of blackspot either more or less severe than indicated by these ratings, they at least will offer a relative scale of blackspot susceptibility.

THE CULTIVARS	COLOR	FORM	HARDINESS ZONE	VIGOR	FRAGRANCE	SEASON	SUITABILITY FOR HEDGING	DISEASE SUSCEPTIBILITY	BREEDER	COUNTRY OF ORIGIN	YEAR INTRODUCED
MISCELLANEOUS SHRUBS (continued)											
Snowdrift	w	d	4	l	f	r	H	BS-2	Lim	USA	2007
William Baffin	dp	s+	2	cl	f	c	H	BS-0	Svejda	Canada	1983
William Booth	mr	s	3	v	f	c		BS-0	Agr. Canada	Canada	1999
Windrush	ly	s+	4	sv	f	r		BS-2	Austin	UK	1985
Winnipeg Parks	dr	d	3	l	f	r	H	BS-2	Agr. Canada	Canada	1993
Zitronenfalter	my	sd	5	sv	ff	r		BS-2	Tantau	Germany	1956

COLOR
w = white or nearly white
p/w = pink and white
pb = pink blend
p/y = pink and yellow
lp = light pink
mp = medium pink
dp = deep pink
mr = medium red
dr = deep red
rb = red blend
m   = mauve
mb = mauve blend
l   = lavender
ly = light yellow
my = medium yellow
dy = deep yellow
yo = yellow-orange
o   = orange
or = orange-red
c/s = coppery salmon

FORM
s   = single
s+ = slightly more than single
sd = semidouble
d   = double
vd = very double or quartered

HARDINESS ZONE
See zone maps on page 178–79.

VIGOR
gc = ground cover
l   = low
sv = semivigorous
v   = vigorous
cl = climber

FRAGRANCE
f   = little or no fragrance
ff   = lightly fragrant
fff = fragrant
ffff = exceptionally fragrant

SEASON
sp = spring
s = summer
r = repeating
c = continuous bloomer

SUITABILITY FOR HEDGING
H = suitable

DISEASE SUSCEPTIBILITY
Mildew:
M = particularly susceptible to mildew

Rust:
R = particularly susceptible to rust

Blackspot:
BS-0 = immune or so little as to be insignificant
BS-1 = noticeable but generally affecting fewer than 25 percent of leaves

BS-2 = affecting at least 50 percent of leaves, some defoliation without protection
BS-3 = affecting most leaves, heavy defoliation without protection

Note: Although roses are subject to several diseases, by far the most important disease of hardy cultivars is blackspot. Those in drier climates may not have problems with blackspot, but in more humid areas blackspot can seriously affect many roses. These designations are based on the incidence of blackspot at a moderately humid site. Although you may find the incidence of blackspot either more or less severe than indicated by these ratings, they at least will offer a relative scale of blackspot susceptibility.

NURSERIES, ORGANIZATIONS AND RESOURCES

NURSERIES

The following nurseries are known to carry hardy roses and, I believe, ship plants. There are doubtless other nurseries that sell hardy roses, and the inclusion of these nurseries is in no way an endorsement of their products.

Adamson's Heritage Nursery
1832 240th Street
Langley, British Columbia V2Z 3A5 Canada
Telephone: 604-530-2476
Fax: 604-530-5886
Website: www.adamsons.ca

The Antique Rose Emporium
10000 FM 50
Brenham, Texas 77833 USA
Telephone: 979-836-5548 (garden center) or 409-836-9051 (mail orders)
Website: www.antiqueroseemporium.com

Corn Hill Nursery Ltd.
2700 Route 890
Corn Hill, New Brunswick E4Z 1M2 Canada
Telephone: 506-756-3635
Website: www.cornhillnursery.com

Greenmantle Nursery
3010 Ettersburg Road
Garberville, California 95542 USA
Telephone: 707-986-7504
Website: www.greenmantlenursery.com

Heirloom Roses
24062 North East Riverside Drive
St. Paul, Oregon 97137 USA
Telephone: 800-820-0465
Website: www.heirloomroses.com

High Country Roses
10195 Wadsworth Boulevard
Broomfield, Colorado 80021 USA
Telephone: 800-552-2082
Website: www.highcountryroses.com

Hortico Nurseries Inc.
422 Concession 5 Road East
Waterdown, Ontario L8B 1K7 Canada
Telephone: 416-689-6984
Website: www.hortico.com

Jackson & Perkins
2 Floral Avenue
Hodges, South Carolina 29653 USA.
Telephone: 888-441-9497
Website: www.jacksonandperkins.com

Morden Nurseries & Garden Centre
P.O. Box 1270
Morden, Manitoba R6M 1B2 Canada
Telephone: 204-325-2254
Fax: 204-325-5763
Website: www.mordennurseries.com

Northland Rosarium
9405 South Williams Lane
Spokane, Washington 99224 USA
Telephone: 509-448-4968
Website: www.northlandrosarium.com

Park Seed Company, Inc.
3507 Cokesbury Road
Hodges, South Carolina 29653 USA
Telephone: 800-845-3369 (toll free) or
864-330-2003 (local)
Website: www.parkseed.com

Roses of Yesterday and Today
803 Brown's Valley Road
Watsonville, California 95076 USA
Telephone: 831-728-1901
Fax: 831-728-0660
Website: www.rosesofyesterday.com

Sheridan Nurseries Ltd.
12302 Tenth Line
Georgetown, Ontario L7G 4S7 Canada
(There are several nursery locations through-
out Ontario)
Telephone: 416-798-7970
Fax: 416-873-2478
Website: www.sheridannurseries.com

ROSE ORGANIZATIONS

The American Rose Society
P.O. Box 30000
Shreveport, Louisiana 71130 USA
Website: www.rose.org

The Canadian Rose Society
233 Covewood Circle NE
Calgary, Alberta T3K 5S7 Canada
Website: www.canadianrosesociety.org

National-Roses-Canada
41 Outer Drive
London, Ontario N6P 1E1 Canada
Telephone: 403-627-2065
Website: www.rosescanada.ca

The Rose Society UK
66 Langer Road
Felixstowe, Suffolk IP112HS UK
+44 1394 670519
Website: www.therosesociety.org.uk

SOURCE BOOKS

There have been innumerable general books written on roses. It would be fruitless to list them all as many are out of print, while others have little information on the hardy roses. The following books are valuable for those seeking more information on hardy roses.

Beales, Peter, *Classic Roses*, Revised Edition, Henry Holt & Co., New York, USA, 1997

Beales, Peter, *Twentieth Century Roses*, Harper & Row Publishers, New York, USA, 1988

Dobson, Beverly and Schneider, Peter, *Combined Rose List*, Peter Schneider, Mantua, USA (Annual list of all rose cultivars in commerce)

Griffiths, Trevor, *The Book of Old Roses*, Penguin Books, New York, USA, 1987

Griffiths, Trevor, *The Book of Classic Old Roses*, Penguin Books, New York, USA, 1988

Krussman, Gerd, *The Complete Book of Roses*, Timber Press, Portland, USA, 1981

McGee, Harry, *The Rosemakers*, National-Roses-Canada, London, Canada, 2010

Ondra, Nancy J., *Taylor's Guide to Roses*, Revised Edition, Houghton Mifflin Harcourt, Boston, USA, 2002

Oster, Maggie, *Taylor's Pocket Guide to Old-Fashioned Roses*, Houghton Mifflin, Boston, USA, 1989

Phillips, Roger and Rix, Martyn, *The Quest for the Rose*, BBC Books, London, UK, 1996

Svejda, Felicitas, *The Canadian Explorer Roses*, National-Roses-Canada, London, Canada, 2008

Thomas, Graham Stewart, *Shrub Roses of Today*, J.M. Dent & Sons, London, UK, 1974

Thomas, Graham Stewart, *The Old Shrub Roses*, J.M. Dent & Sons, London, UK, 1978

Verrier, Suzanne, *Rosa rugosa*, Firefly Books, Richmond Hill, Canada, 1999

Verrier, Suzanne, *Rosa gallica*, Firefly Books, Richmond Hill, Canada, 1999

Young, Marily (author, ed.), Schorr, Phillip (author) and Baer, Rich (illustrator), *Modern Roses 12*, American Rose Society, Shreveport, USA, 2007 (A list of all registered roses and roses of historical or botanical importance)

INDEX